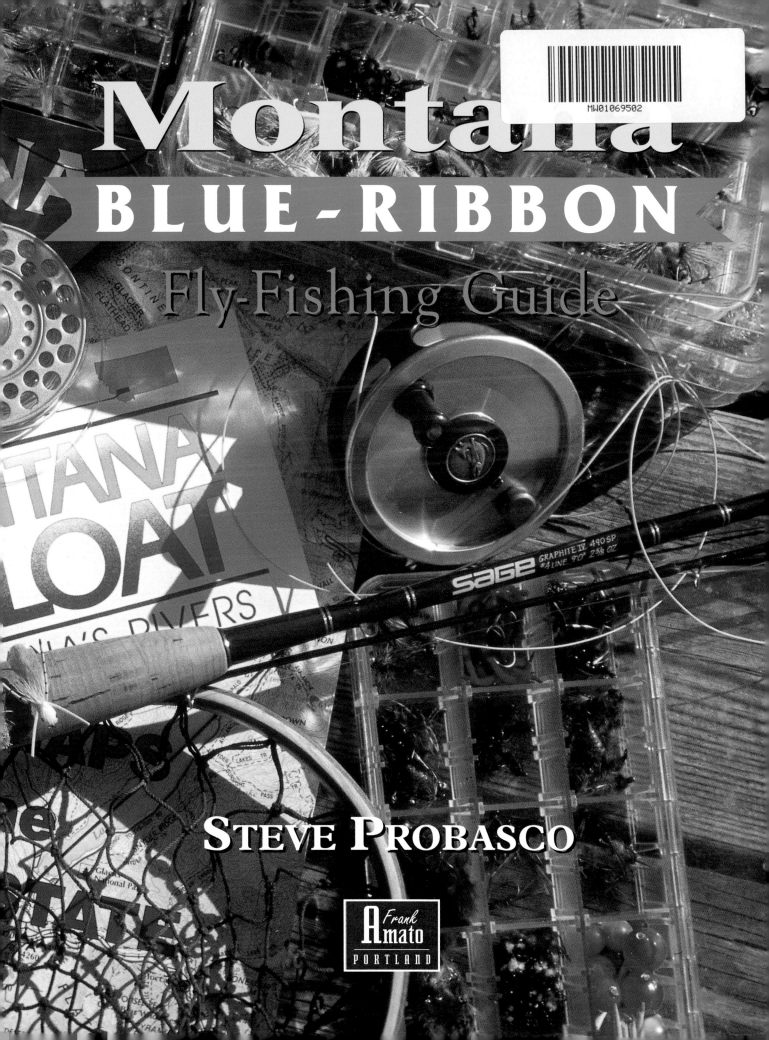

Montana
BLUE-RIBBON
Fly-Fishing Guide

STEVE PROBASCO

Frank Amato
PORTLAND

Acknowledgments

I would like to thank all of my friends who so diligently followed me to Montana while doing "research" for this book. A special thanks to Umpqua Feather Merchants of Glide, Oregon (541) 496-3512 for providing all the flies for the fly plate.

About the Author

Steve Probasco has been an angling writer and photographer for the past two decades. His articles and photographs have appeared in a host of publications. Steve is the author of ten fly-fishing books, and one video on fly tying, with several other works in progress. He makes his home with his family in Raymond, Washington.

Published in 2000 by Frank Amato Publications, Inc.
P.O. Box 82112, Portland, Oregon 97282
(503) 653-8108 • www.amatobooks.com

Softbound ISBN: 1-57188-165-4
Softbound UPC: 0-66066-00363-8

All photographs taken by Steve Probasco except where noted.

Book Design: Amy Tomlinson

Printed in Thailand

1 3 5 7 9 10 8 6 4 2

Montana

BLUE-RIBBON

Fly-Fishing Guide

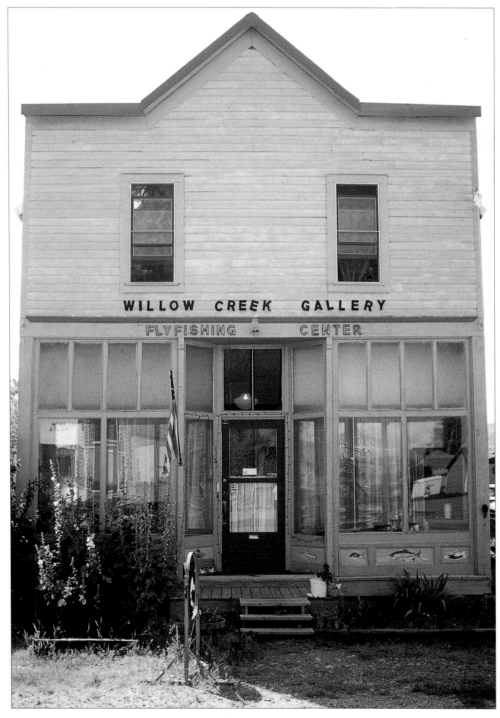

STEVE PROBASCO

TABLE OF
Contents

Montana Map

—— 6 ——

Introduction

—— 8 ——

WESTERN
Montana

1 Kootenai River
2 Flathead River
3 Middle Fork Flathead
4 North Fork Flathead
5 South Fork Flathead
6 Flathead Lake
7 Hungry Horse Reservoir
8 Swan River
9 Metcalf Lake
10 Yaak River
11 Clark Fork River
12 Lolo Creek
13 St. Regis River
14 Thompson River
15 Jocko River
16 Rock Creek
17 Bitterroot River
18 Blackfoot River
19 Little Blackfoot River
20 Anaconda Settling Ponds
21 Blackfeet Reservation Lakes: Duck, Mission, Mitten, Kipp, Four Horn, Dog Gun
22 Georgetown Lake
23 Flint Creek
24 Flathead Indian Reservation
25 Glacier National Park

CENTRAL
Montana

1 Big Hole River
2 Beaverhead River
3 Grasshopper Creek
4 Poindexter Slough
5 Clark Canyon Reservoir
6 Red Rock River
7 Jefferson River
8 Ruby River

9 Missouri River
10 Little Prickly Pear Creek
11 Canyon Ferry Reservoir
12 Sun River
13 Smith River
14 Marias River
15 Madison River
16 South Fork Madison River

Montana
BLUE-RIBBON STREAMS & LAKES

Traveling light for a week of Montana fishing.

Introduction

Montana. Just saying the word conjures up visions of powerful rivers and meandering trout streams, cowboys and Indians, the Rocky Mountains and wide-open spaces. Montana is *the* destination in the lower 48 for the serious fly-fisher. Sure, there are other great places to fly-fish around the country, but Montana is the core—a magnet, drawing anglers like gravity sucks an apple from a tree.

Some of the most famous rivers in the world gouge Montana's surface. It would be hard to find a fly-fisher anywhere who hasn't heard of such waters as the Madison, Yellowstone, Bighorn, Big Hole, Beaverhead and a host of others made famous by angling legends and fly-fishing writers. Montana is blessed with a plethora of rivers, streams and lakes—a fly-fisher's paradise.

The biggest problem with fly-fishing Montana is deciding just where to go. How do you spend your valuable vacation time? How many rivers can you squeeze in? How do you get the most bang for your buck?

Many anglers, especially first-timers, head for Montana with plans of doing it all. Montana is a big place. Overzealous ambition usually leads to frustration and disappointment. I know...I've been there. It's best to just concentrate your efforts in a small geographical area. In Montana it's easy to do this and still fish several quality waters in a week's time.

Even though the word "Montana" is synonymous with wild rivers and big trout, this state is not without its problems. Before the popular outburst of fly-fishing, and before clean water and common sense about our environment became a big deal, before Montana became a destination state for visiting anglers, and before tourism became the most valuable industry in the state, Montana's magnificent waters were looked at as nothing more than irrigation for ranchers and a place to dump mining waste. No consideration was given to poor logging practices. Jobs had priority. Period. As sad and short-sighted as this was, it still goes on today. There is still a battle between consumptive interests and common sense, between lawmakers and those who actually care about this planet; the save-it-before-it's-gone crowd that find themselves pounding their heads against the wall, pleading reality and sure-sense to apathetic ears. Montana has a long way to go. Let's hope it gets there before it's too late.

Whew, glad I got that off my chest!

This book is not intended to be the definitive guide to fly-fishing Montana. Obviously, every single fishery the state has to offer wouldn't fit in just one volume. The intention of this book is to share with you Montana's best waters—the "blue-ribbon" streams and lakes that have made the "Big Sky Country" so famous. But I encourage you to explore more waters than those you read about here. Take the back roads, fish the smaller streams and ask permission to fish on private lands; Montana has much to offer those with the incentive and a persistence to seek it out.

So, let's go. Turn the page and let me share with you some of Montana's blue-ribbon waters.

Steve Probasco
Raymond, WA

WESTERN Montana

Western Montana is blessed with a plethora of trout streams, rivers and lakes. It is the least-fished part of Montana, not because the fishing isn't as good as in other parts but, perhaps, because the most famous and publicized waters in the state (in the United States, for that matter) are located to the east, in the Yellowstone area.

Just beyond the Idaho border, the Bitterroot Mountains stretch nearly the entire length of the state, creating a personality and specific character unlike that found in the rest of Montana. The Bitterroots suck Pacific moisture from the sky like a sponge. Western Montana, for definition, is that part of Montana located west of the Continental Divide, therefore draining into the Pacific Ocean. This part of Montana receives considerably more moisture than any other part of the state.

Because of the moisture, western Montana is densely timbered, the northwestern portion the heaviest, as this region gets the most rain. During winter this translates into a significant snowpack during most years. Cool mountain streams are the result during summer, and western Montana hosts an abundance of small trout waters that beg for the wading angler.

Much of western Montana is National Forest land making stream access very easy. Pulling over your car, pulling on your waders and slipping into the stream is commonplace.

Many of the streams in western Montana host the native, Westslope cutthroat trout, one of the prettiest and most voracious feeding trout in the West. And where cutthroat are found, many times there are also bull trout. Endangered in many areas, bull trout of enormous proportions will hold in the deepest of pools. It is a rush indeed to be playing in a 12-inch cutthroat and have it attacked by a three-foot bull trout!

Western Montana is the state's least fished, and possibly its best-kept secret. It is certainly a region worth exploring, for all its wonders.

Sunrise at Duck Lake (Blackfeet Reservation).

Kootenai River

With its beginnings on the west slope of the Canadian Rockies, the Kootenai River takes a dip into Montana and Idaho before turning north again and completing its journey to the Columbia River back in Canada. In Montana, Libby Dam, above which is found Lake Koocanusa, a large impoundment that stretches into Canada, blocks the Kootenai. Simply by its location, the Kootenai is not in the "hub" of Montana fly-fishing, but it's a tremendous river, certainly worthy of the attention of fly-fishers.

There is some prime fly-fishing found in the upper, Canadian reaches of the Kootenai, but the best fly-fishing to be had in the river in Montana is the stretch from Libby Dam downstream to Kootenai Falls, a distance just shy of 30 miles. Long, wide runs, side-channels, deep pools and powerful flows characterize the tailwater section of this river.

Streamers should always be included in your Montana arsenal.

The Kootenai has a reputation for kicking out some pretty impressive fish. Rainbow trout approaching 30 pounds have been taken below the dam. These are fish feeding on chum from Kokanee and trout that pass through the power-generating turbines. Mostly they are taken by meat-fishermen, but there is an increasing number of fly-anglers who test their nerve and tackle on these brutes. Hi-D sinking lines and duck-and-chuck heads, big streamers and patience are needed if you are to have a shot at these fish.

Most of the rainbows fall far short of those leviathans found below the dam feeding on chum. That's not to say you can't catch big fish elsewhere in the Kootenai—you can, it's just that they will be a more "normal" kind of big. There are plenty of five-pounders available, but the average rainbow will run one to two pounds.

During peak power generation and during runoff, which occurs from late April into August, the Kootenai can flow as high as 30,000 cfs. I'm told the best float-fishing takes place when flows are less than 12,000 cfs. The river is impossible to wade and very dangerous at flows above 7,000 cfs. Even at ideal wading flows of around 4,000 cfs, the Kootenai is a big river that demands plenty of common sense, and a whole lot of respect.

If planning to float this river, words of caution are in order. There are some definite hazards to avoid. Downstream from Libby, China Rapids is encountered and should only be attempted by experienced floaters. It is a must to scout this rapid before attempting it. Just below China Rapids lies Kootenai Falls. You must exit the river before the falls (there is a take-out just above the falls) as it is not floatable by anyone. The river remains wild until it reaches the town of Troy. With the exception of the confluence of the Yaak River, the Kootenai is pretty mellow all the way to the Idaho border.

The Kootenai sees sporadic hatches of *Baetis* and midges before the high water of spring. Consistent hatches don't appear until June, after the water has warmed. Blue-winged olives, iron duns and the Grannom caddis are the first major hatches, followed by pale morning duns and spotted sedges later on. Hoppers provide some fast action along the edges during late summer, and large streamers are a favorite in the deeper water.

The Kootenai should be approached with a variety of tackle. Most of the summer fishing can be accomplished with a 5- to 6-weight rod and a floating line. However, if you are monster hunting, a 7- to 8-weight rod and heavy shooting heads are a good idea for working big streamers down deep.

Access to the upper Kootenai is good. State Route 37 and U.S. Route 2 parallel the river. Access below Kootenai Falls is not as good, as much of the surrounding land is private.

A good contact when planning a trip to the Kootenai is Dave Blackburn at the Kootenai Angler, 13546 Highway 37, Libby, MT 59923, (406) 293-7578.

Flathead River

The main stem Flathead River is born to the east of Columbia Falls at a point where the North Fork and Middle Fork merge at Blankenship Bridge. The South Fork joins downstream, as does the Whitefish, Stillwater and Swan rivers along the Flathead's 55-mile course to Flathead Lake. Needless to say, this is big water. Westslope cutthroat, rainbow and bull trout, and whitefish are all found here.

The upper river can be accessed at Blankenship Bridge, and at a couple other points, but possibly the best access is at

Westslope cutthroat from the South Fork of the Flathead River.

the mouth of the Stillwater River, near Kalispell. From here anglers can work a 10-mile section of river.

Many anglers prefer to float the Flathead, floating it is fairly straightforward but floaters need to keep in mind the power of big rivers. Beware of strong eddies.

Big streamers and nymphs, as well as a variety of dries, will take trout here. The key when fishing big water like the Flathead is to break the river down into smaller chunks and fish those chunks as you would a smaller stream.

Below Flathead Lake the river changes face. Below Kerr Dam, there are still some cutthroat, browns and rainbows, but the water gets warmer as it flows downstream toward its confluence with the Clark Fork. Northern pike and largemouth bass thrive in this section of river. This section of river flows through the Flathead Indian Reservation, requiring a tribal permit to fish. Access is not all that good, but can be found at a few points along Highway 200, and near Dixon.

Pike can be found hiding along the weed beds and gravel bars and can be taken on nearly any large streamer. Rabbit-strip patterns in red, orange, yellow, white and black, and in sizes 2/0 to 4/0 work well, and will survive the pike's razor-sharp teeth. Largemouth bass can be found in lesser numbers in sloughs adjoining the river.

Middle Fork Flathead River

The Middle Fork of the Flathead River comes to life in the Great Bear Wilderness, eventually following U.S. 2 along the southwestern border of Glacier National Park. It is the section of river located in the wilderness area that offers the best fishing. Access is by foot, horse or plane.

Floating the river obviously puts the angler on more water, but logistics of getting into the wilderness is a plan in itself. Some floaters fly into a headwaters' landing strip to begin their float. However, some of the float travels through a canyon, and under certain flows can be dangerous to all but experienced rafters. Packing in has its own merits, and access is good from trails that lead up the river.

The Westslope cutthroat found in the wilderness can reach 20 inches or better and will attack nearly any properly presented dry fly. Bull trout will attack a cutthroat you are playing, or a large streamer worked through the deepest holes. Be careful to release these fish unharmed, in fact, release all your fish unharmed—it's simply the right thing to do.

Once the Middle Fork leaves the wilderness, the fishing drops off considerably. Above West Glacier, the river is more of a whitewater-rafting affair than a fishing destination.

North Fork Flathead

With its beginnings in British Columbia, the North Fork flows along the western border of Glacier National Park to join the Middle Fork and form the main stem Flathead River. Access is good via the North Fork Road, which parallels the river. The view into Glacier National Park is stunning.

Of the three forks of the Flathead, the North Fork is the least targeted by serious anglers. Cutthroat here average smaller than in the other forks, but they are plentiful and will smack just about any fly floated their way. Bull trout can be found in the deeper pools and runs, some of which can push 20 pounds.

South Fork Flathead

Of the three forks of the Flathead River, the South Fork is probably the most noted fishery. This is due, in part, to the fact that it is the hardest to get to. For roughly 50 miles the

South Fork travels through the Bob Marshall Wilderness; probably the most remote, unspoiled chunk of real estate in the lower 48.

The Westslope cutthroat fishery of the South Fork is arguably the best in the state. Above Hungry Horse Reservoir the river quickly winds into the Bob Marshall Wilderness. Access is by a select few points along the road on the lower reaches, and by foot or horseback once you get into the wilderness. Several local outfitters in the Whitefish and Kalispell area offer horse and rafting trips.

The cutthroat in the South Fork can reach 20 inches or better, and the bull trout that migrate up this little, crystal-clear stream can reach 20 pounds. Nearly any high-floating dry fly will take the cutthroat, and streamers worked through the deepest pools will sometimes provoke the bull trout.

None of the forks of the Flathead are rich in aquatic life, as their waters mostly come from snowmelt. Mayflies, caddis, stoneflies and midges are all present, but do not provide crazy hatches or feeding frenzies like on many other Montana rivers. Food is precious here, and fish don't pass up anything that looks like calories. Don't overlook terrestrials like ants, bees and beetles.

Flathead Lake

From its outward appearance, Flathead Lake looks like it would have little to offer the fly angler. This is big water. In fact, Flathead Lake is the largest body of fresh water west of the Mississippi. It is mostly known as a downrigger fishery for lake trout but it does have a few things to offer the fly-fisher.

Lake whitefish are abundant in Flathead Lake. These are large specimens—many mature fish are over five pounds. They can be taken on flies, especially during fall when they school in the shallow bays around the lake. Sinking lines and size 10 to 12 nymphs like the Pheasant Tail and Gold Ribbed Hare's Ear will take whitefish once you have located them.

Lake trout can also be taken on large streamers during the fall when they cruise the shorelines. Those same bays where you will find the whitefish are the place to look for the lakers. Streamers should be big—size 4 or larger!

At times, cutthroat and bull trout will be feeding on hatching insects, and if you are there at the right time you can get in on the action. Again, it is the bays where you should concentrate your fishing, especially bays where streams enter the lake.

There is a threat in Flathead Lake from illegally planted fish, such as northern pike, largemouth bass, yellow perch and the threat of the introduction of walleye. The problem is that these fish not only compete for the foods of the native fish, some of them, like the northern pike, eat them. A lot of them!

The problem with accidental or illegal planting of non-native fish is that it can throw a natural ecosystem out of whack. Entire fisheries have been lost because of this. Please report violators if you ever see it happen.

Opposite page: The Swan River during fall.

Access is good, with highways all around the lake. Camping is available in many established parks along the lake's shore. The south end of Flathead Lake is within the boundaries of the Flathead Indian Reservation—tribal permits are needed.

Hungry Horse Reservoir

With Glacier National Park to the north, the Bob Marshall Wilderness to the south and the Great Bear Wilderness to the east, Hungry Horse Reservoir is surrounded by some pretty significant real estate. When the Hungry Horse Dam was built back in 1953, it was the fourth largest dam in the world. With the building of the dam, 34 miles of the South Fork Flathead River were forever changed.

Although the fishery that was destroyed was replaced by another, albeit unnatural and not nearly as pretty, Hungry Horse Reservoir does offer some angling to fly-fishers. This 22,000-acre reservoir hosts a healthy population of cutthroat, bull trout and whitefish.

Most of the fly angling on the reservoir is done in the bays near tributary streams. There is little shoreline fishing here, and the standard method for fly-casters is to anchor a small boat off the mouths of streams and cast towards shore. Both cutthroat and bull trout can be caught in this manner.

Especially good during spring are the stream mouths for the pre-spawn cutthroat, and again during fall for the pre-spawn bull trout. However, the reservoir can be productive for the exploring angler from spring through fall.

Standard attractor dry flies like the Humpy, Royal Trude, and Bivisible are effective for the cutthroat. Rods in the 4- to 5-weight range are adequate, floating lines and fine leaders will get you into fish. Bull trout require a rod with a little more spunk, a 6- or 7-weight is much better. Large streamers are the ticket for these aggressive fighters.

Hungry Horse Reservoir is located just off Highway 2, near the town of Hungry Horse. A gravel road surrounds the reservoir providing access. Camping is available in the area.

Swan River

The Swan River's origins are in the mountains to the west of the Bob Marshall Wilderness. Beginning as the outflow of Lindbergh Lake, the Swan flows roughly 30 miles to Swan Lake, just to the east of big Flathead Lake.

Rainbow, cutthroat, brook and bull trout are all found here, but it is the cutthroat that are most plentiful. Although not huge fish, they are willing to take dry flies and, at times, can be caught in numbers. There is a strong spawning run of bull trout that move up from Swan Lake. However, deliberately fishing for them is a violation, as these are protected fish.

Various mayfly, caddis and stoneflies are found in the Swan. High-floating dries like the Humpy, Elk Hair Caddis and Parachute Adams in sizes 12 to 14 are good choices.

Public access is good, as Highway 83 runs along the east side of the stream. However, brushy banks make for a lot of

Ready for the fall browns.

Another exciting time to be on this water is during the damselfly migration from mid-June into July. Any damsel nymph fished slowly under the surface will produce well. Intermediate sinking lines are ideal for this type of fishing.

By fall, when the water cools down some, trout will again become active. This is a good time to work the drop-offs and other structure with Woolly Buggers and other streamers.

To reach the lake, take the Fatty Creek Road off Highway 83. If this dirt road is wet, a 4WD vehicle will be a bonus. Access is down a steep bank on the north side of the lake. For this reason, float tubes and small personal boats are the best crafts to use here.

Yaak River

The North Fork of the Yaak flows from the mountains of southern British Columbia into Montana, where the East Fork of the Yaak joins. The West Fork joins the East Fork and the main stem Yaak is born.

Clear-cut logging has been the enemy of this river for some time. Sediment from the clear-cuts and logging roads inevitably filter into the river and tributaries, choking the life out of every living thing. Still, in the fighting fashion of many Montana streams, the Yaak remains a good fly-fishing stream—not what it could be, but good nonetheless.

The North Fork holds a native strain of rainbows that are on the small size, there are not many of them and access is poor. The West Fork holds small cutthroat, and being bordered by Forest Service land, access is good. The East Fork holds a decent population of brook trout, and a big one will be a foot or so long. Access to the East Fork is also good.

After all the forks join, the main stem Yaak becomes a medium-sized stream. Not surprisingly, it is the main stem Yaak that holds the largest trout. The best fishing is above Yaak Falls, four miles above the river's confluence with the Kootenai. The river flows through a canyon, difficult to access and difficult to fish, but holds the best trout. To reach it you can walk upstream from the Highway 2 crossing or brave the canyon wall down to the river.

Grizzly bears are a factor to consider when fishing parts of Montana.

bushwhacking and frustration. The best fishing, like in many streams, is the farthest you can walk from the easiest access points.

An unimproved campground is located near Fatty Creek, which is located near the Swan's middle section.

Metcalf Lake

Metcalf is a small, 13-acre lake located 14 miles south of Swan Lake, reached via Highway 83. Although not a large piece of water, this little lake kicks out some awfully big rainbows. Trout in the 20s (inches) regularly come from this lake.

Spring and fall are the best times to fish Metcalf Lake. The summer months are simply too warm. Trout can still be taken but you must fish down deep, and painstakingly slowly. The best spot during the heat of summer is on the north end where there are some underwater springs.

Fishing gets underway after ice-off in spring when midges are hatching. Size 16 midge pupas work well, as do small adult midge imitations. Fish the shallows, and follow the path of cruising fish. Sight-fishing for big rainbows with tiny midges is an adrenaline junkie's ultimate fix.

Fishing above the canyon is also good, with rainbows and brook trout to 20 inches. Perhaps the biggest draw on the Yaak is the stretch of river above Pete Creek. Here the river becomes a meadow stream that holds mostly brook trout—some reaching five pounds. Streamers are the ticket here for the bigger fish.

For the most part, the Yaak is a dry fly and wading stream. The fish in this river respond well to the variety of mayflies and caddis that hatch all season long. A day spent walking the banks of the Yaak often ends with dozens of trout hooked and released.

To reach the Yaak River follow Highway 2 northwest from Libby and turn right on the Yaak River Road. Oh yeah, keep an eye out for grizzly bears when fishing the Yaak!

Clark Fork River

History tells us over and over again how consumptive interests overrule common sense and respect for our natural resources. The Clark Fork River has been victimized more than its share, and is still trying to recover from blatant disregard in the name of cold hard cash.

The river's headwaters are located in mining country. Slag piles (toxic mine tailings) are often washed into Silver Bow Creek, the headwater stream of the Clark Fork which, as of this writing, is not clean enough to support trout. Environmental pressure resulted in the Anaconda settling ponds, a series of shallow ponds treated to minimize toxic metals in the water. The outlet of the ponds is now the official start of the Clark Fork, and the outflow is clean enough to support brown trout. However, it is still too polluted to support the other trout species.

Downstream from the settling ponds, the Clark Fork suffers from the same kind of problems, and more. Cloudbursts cause toxins to be washed into the river causing massive fish kills every few years. Toxins that have accumulated behind Milltown Dam, seven miles east of Missoula, are a disaster waiting to happen. In addition to the pollution problems, parts of the Clark Fork face severe de-watering problems from irrigation demands. As a result, high water temperatures stress and kill the trout populations. This is especially significant from the town of Drummond to the mouth of Rock Creek.

Despite all the atrocities and neglect that Rock Creek seems to endure, this is still one of Montana's best trout fisheries. Fragile, and a time bomb, yes, but still a tremendous fishery.

Brown trout dominate the upper Clark Fork downstream from the Anaconda settling ponds to Milltown Dam near Missoula. A few large rainbows can also be caught in this section, but it is the brown trout that draws the anglers—brown trout and the incredible caddis hatches that are found here. During the heat of the hatch, caddis clouds are mind-boggling. A rust-colored Elk Hair Caddis in size 12 to 16 works well at times but LaFontaine's Emergent Sparkle Pupa in the same sizes will definitely take more fish. Brushy, undercut banks, riffles and pools make the upper Clark Fork a dry-fly paradise.

Fishing the Clark Fork from a personal boat.

Be prepared with a variety of fly patterns when traveling to Montana waters.

Lightning storms are common during summer.

Below the confluence of Rock Creek and the Clark Fork, downstream to Milltown Dam, more cleaner water produces a mixture of brown and rainbow trout. Mayfly hatches become more important from here downstream. Also significant is the salmonfly hatch that occurs in mid to late May.

Downstream from Milltown Dam and the confluence of the Blackfoot River, the Clark Fork is a big river. Major tributaries contribute strength downstream including such notable rivers as the Bitterroot, Thompson, Flathead and more. Rainbow, brown and cutthroat trout share this water with whitefish and bull trout. Mayfly hatches are regular, and include most of the major western species including PMDs, gray drakes, green drakes, Tricos, *Baetis*, etc. Simply put, the fly-fisher should go prepared with a variety of mayfly imitations in a variety of sizes. Stoneflies, as well as terrestrials (especially hoppers), can be important at times also.

Many anglers float the lower river and give most of their attention to the numerous riffles, banks and current seams that concentrate aquatic insects and other food items. Personal boats, rafts and drift boats all work well on most of the lower Clark Fork. The entire river is floatable but drops into a narrow canyon west of Alberton. Only experienced boaters should attempt this stretch of water.

Access to most of the Clark Fork is good. The upper river, and much of the lower river, is paralleled by Interstate 90, with numerous side roads and bridge crossings. Many developed access sites are found along the Clark Fork, as are campgrounds and other services. Several fly shops can be found in Missoula and in Butte.

Lolo Creek

Lolo Creek flows from the mountains on the Idaho-Montana border, not too far south of Missoula. Careless logging practices have taken their toll here, and although this pretty little stream is filled with plenty of rainbow, cutthroat, brook and brown trout, none of them get very big. Still, it is a fun little stream to fish.

A variety of mayflies and caddis hatch here, and the dry-fly enthusiast can spend the day taking numbers of trout from Lolo's generous waters. This is 3-weight heaven.

Larger fish are often caught during spring and fall when spawning rainbows and browns move up this tributary from the Bitterroot River.

Access to Lolo Creek is good, as Highway 12 parallels the creek for approximately 30 miles. To reach Highway 12, follow Highway 93 south from Missoula for 15 miles.

St. Regis River

Driving into Montana from Idaho, the first Montana river you lay eyes on is the St. Regis. It begins near Lookout Pass and flows for 35 miles to the Clark Fork River. The St. Regis is a beautiful little stream, during the low-water season of late summer and fall you can nearly hop across it in places. A 20-foot cast will land your fly in the trees of the far bank.

As pretty as this little river is, it's not what you would call a prime destination for most of the season. At one time it was, but that was pre-Interstate 90. Interstate 90 parallels the river for its entire length, and during construction the St. Regis suffered greatly.

Still, things are improving, and smallish cutthroat and brook trout can be had throughout the river, which presents very clear, with riffles, pools and bends. There is always the chance of a larger fish, possibly a rainbow from the deepest pools and undercut banks. Attractor patterns work well here; Humpies, Royal Trudes, etc., as do the standard Adams and Elk Hair Caddis.

Where the St. Regis does shine is during the spring and fall in the lower river near its confluence with the Clark Fork. In spring, rainbows migrate up the St. Regis to spawn. During fall it's the brown trout that make the journey. Fishing streamers is a good technique for both species.

Access to the St. Regis is off Interstate 90 all along its route.

Thompson River

The Thompson begins as the outflow from Lower Thompson Lake, west of Kalispell. It ends roughly 50 miles distant when it empties into the Clark Fork River. Throughout its length, the Thompson is a good fly-fishing stream. No, you won't find monster "Montana" trout here, but you will find brook, rainbow, brown, cutthroat and bull trout in this smallish river.

In its upper reaches the Thompson winds through meadows where small cutthroat and brookies are found. Then the river travels through a canyon before opening up some as it completes its journey to the Clark Fork. It is this section of the Thompson where the largest fish are found.

A variety of mayflies, stoneflies and caddis hatch throughout the season, and hoppers are available during late summer and fall. Anglers should arrive "prepared." Being a "cast-across" river, the Thompson is a great dry-fly stream.

Getting there can be half the challenge. Summer can bring serious thunderstorms.

Above: Brown trout.
Opposite page: Nymphing the pocket water of middle Rock Creek.

Access is good here, with dirt roads paralleling the river for most of its length. Although clear most of the time, sediment from logging is a problem and increases egg mortality. This is the "little river that could" if logging was practiced responsibly, poachers were shot in their tracks and fishing regulations took a responsible approach to management.

Jocko River

The Jocko River begins at the outlet of Lower Jocko Lake. The river gains force after the South and Middle Forks enter. The main stem Jocko flows about 20 miles from its forks to join the Flathead River at Dixon. U.S. 93 follows the Jocko for much of its fishable length.

The entire river flows through the Flathead Indian Reservation and a permit is required to fish. Although not a long river, the Jocko can be an interesting side-trip.

Downstream from where Highway 93 crosses the river is the easiest to fish. Here you will find brown, rainbow, brook, cutthroat and bull trout, as well as plenty of whitefish. This is good dry fly and nymph water. You can't go wrong with an Elk Hair Caddis, Adams or a Humpy in sizes 12 to 16.

A word of caution: if your are a bit squeamish or flat-out afraid of rattlesnakes you best not fish here because there are plenty!

Rock Creek

If you come to Rock Creek looking for a "creek" you will be disappointed. Rock Creek is actually a small river. Labeled blue-ribbon by the state, Rock Creek is one of western Montana's best trout waters. Here you can find diversity hard to match. Rainbow, brown, cutthroat, brook and bull trout can all be found here.

Rock Creek comes to life at the base of the Sapphire Mountains, at the confluence of the East and West Fork, flowing mostly through private property, the upper reaches consist of riffled water and flats as it winds through a wide valley. Cutthroat and brook trout are predominate, with the occasional rainbow sometimes caught. As in most upper reaches, the trout are not monsters here. A 12-incher is a prize.

From the point where Big Hogback Creek enters, Rock Creek takes on a completely different appearance. From here, down to Harry's Flat Campground the river is faster, with less holding water and rainbows outnumber the other species. Working downstream the trout get larger, and in this section you can expect to find the occasional fish of 20 inches or more. Access is great, as the Rock Creek Road winds along the river with numerous pullovers.

Camping along Rock Creek.

Tim Mondale nymphing the pocket water in "The Dalles" section of Rock Creek.

The area know as "The Dalles" is a heavily-bouldered, narrow stretch of water that is spectacularly beautiful, but surrenders few fish. Trout in the deep, slow water of this boulder garden are tough to get at. Heavily-weighted nymphs drifted along the bottom and around the rocks are your best bet for making contact. Some hefty rainbows, browns and bull trout come from this section for the patient and determined angler.

From the Dalles downstream, Rock Creek has the kind of trout diversity that has made this little river famous. Here anglers can find rainbow and brown trout hiding in all the likely places—riffles, logjams, pools, undercut banks, etc. The further downstream you get, brown trout become more prevalent. Some of these browns can be truly large, especially during fall when spawning fish migrate up from the Clark Fork River.

Rock Creek is a very rich stream. Insect hatches are reliable and heavy. April brings a hatch of March browns to die for, but it is the giant salmonfly (*Pteronarcys californica*) that draws anglers when they appear from late May through June during spring runoff. As in other rivers hosting the salmonfly hatch, Rock Creek becomes crowded during the hatch. This is one time when boating anglers have an advantage over the wading angler. If you do float though, keep in mind that this is a fast, potentially dangerous stream during runoff because of sweepers and logjams. Also keep in mind it is closed to fishing from boats from July 1 through November 30.

During the salmonfly hatch, anglers attack this little river with flies big enough to choke a horse. Trout become accustomed to seeing plenty of phony bugs floating by—and persistent anglers can get rises from Orange Stimulators and the like—but more effective in this off-colored water is a size 2 or size 4 stonefly nymph bounced along the bottom on a 2X or 3X tippet. This works well before, during and after the hatch. After the salmonfly hatch, the hoards of anglers disappear as quickly as they came.

When runoff is over and the water clears, Rock Creek becomes one of the most pleasant little streams to wade and cast a dry fly or nymph that you can imagine. Other summer and fall hatches include a variety of smaller stoneflies, caddis, pale morning duns, *Baetis* and midges. Terrestrials such as grasshoppers and ants are productive throughout the summer, as are spruce moths if you are present when they appear in August. Late fall streamer fishing in the lower river near the confluence with the Clark Fork can be spectacular.

Rock Creek is reached via the Rock Creek Road, 20 miles east of Missoula, off Interstate 90. A gravel road follows Rock Creek for much of its fishable length. Several Forest Service campgrounds are located along the river. Upper Rock Creek

A chunky Rock Creek rainbow comes to net.

can be reached by following this road or via Highway 38 from Philipsburg.

Rock Creek Mercantile (406) 825-6440, located on the lower Rock Creek Road, is a full-service fly shop with plenty of tackle, flies and most importantly—information.

A young bull moose along Rock Creek.

Bitterroot River

The Bitterroot Mountains rise to the west, their sheer granite walls tantalizing any rock climber who catches a glimpse. To the east, the Sapphire Mountains form the other boundary of the valley through which the Bitterroot River flows. This is one of the prettiest places in Montana.

The West Fork of the Bitterroot River begins in the mountains near the Idaho-Montana border. It is joined by the East Fork, which originates in the Anaconda-Pintler Wilderness, near Conner, then flows over 70 miles to its confluence with the Clark Fork River, west of Missoula.

The Bitterroot ecosystem is not as rich as some Montana rivers further to the east, and it never will be. However, rainbow, cutthroat, brook, brown and bull trout, as well as the ever-present in Montana whitefish, can all be taken. Some fish may go 20 inches or more. Most will be smaller.

This river is equally popular with floaters and waders. Good access along its length allows both to spread out so consequently the Bitterroot is seldom crowded—at least not like some Montana rivers.

The Bitterroot is blessed with consistent and regular hatches of mayflies, caddisflies and stoneflies. Not the blizzard hatches found in some places, but consistent, nonetheless. Perhaps the most significant single hatch on the Bitterroot is the Skwala stoneflies which occur in March and April. Anglers come out of the woodwork for this hatch, but seem to dissipate as soon as it's over.

Stonefly nymphs.

When the Skwalas are present, a size 8, dark-olive stonefly nymph is hard to beat. If you are stuck on dry-fly fishing, a size 8 olive Stimulator will take its share of trout.

Seasonal hatches of mayflies include PMDs, green drakes, brown drakes, *Baetis* and Tricos. Various caddis and stoneflies, including golden stones, appear, as do hoppers in the

Opposite page: Angling in upper Rock Creek.
Below: Not all Montana rainbows are trophy-sized, but they are all beautiful.

late summer and fall. The bottom line here is, when traveling to the Bitterroot bring a well-stocked fly box and be prepared for whatever hatch happens to be at the time.

The lower Bitterroot suffers from irrigation draw-down during dry summers which impacts not only the fish but also your ability to float. It is wise to check out the river before you toss your boat in. If you do float the river be aware of the diversion dams; do your homework!

Access to the entire Bitterroot is from various bridges and public access points along Highway 93. All amenities are found along Highway 93, including camping, motels, restaurants, etc.

Blackfoot River

It wouldn't be right to speak of the Blackfoot River without mentioning Norman McLean's book, *A River Runs Through It*, which was made into a major motion picture released in 1992. The setting of the book was the Blackfoot River during the earlier part of this century. It was too bad that much of the filming had to be done elsewhere, as the Blackfoot had fallen victim to the selfish, consumptive practices of man; logging, mining, and poor ranching practices.

Shortly after the film was released, the environmental group, American Rivers, placed the Blackfoot on its 10 most endangered rivers list. The Blackfoot gained a new following of "friends" determined to rectify the blatant and careless disregard for this natural resource. But the consumptive lobby dollars speak loudly, and as of this writing, this beautiful 130-mile long Montana river's future is still hanging by a thread. Another major mine is being planned in the headwaters.

The Blackfoot River begins in the mountains near the Continental Divide. It flows in a southwesterly direction, and joins the Clark Fork River near Bonner. Highway 200 follows the Blackfoot for much of its length providing good access to most of the river.

Even though the Blackfoot has had its ups and downs over the years, today, parts of the river are on an upward trend. This is probably due to the fact that in 1990, the Blackfoot became catch-and-release for cutthroat and bull trout, and slot limits were placed on rainbow and brown trout—fish over 12 inches had to be released. Now, the Blackfoot kicks out fish trout to 20-inches or more.

From the rivers source down to Lincoln, the Blackfoot is unproductive due to mine sediments. From Lincoln, down to near the point where the North Fork enters, fishing picks up. Brown trout are predominate, as they can better survive the mining secretions. Some of these browns are good-sized, and although a brushy place to fish, a Girdle Bug drifted into a logjam can produce some exciting results. Downstream from the North Fork, with cleaner water entering, the mainstem Blackfoot turns into a classic Western trout stream, and holds browns, rainbows, cutthroat, brookies, and bull trout.

Like on many Montana rivers, fishing gets underway on the Blackfoot before the spring runoff. Skwala stoneflies are the major attraction from late March through April. Adult patterns

Opposite page: Bitterroot River.

Fall colors along the Blackfoot River.

are exciting, but as in most cases, not nearly as productive as the nymphs. *Baetis* hatches occur during this time also, and size 16 olive adult imitations are the standard during this hatch.

Spring runoff usually begins by mid-May, virtually shutting down the fishing for awhile. Salmonflies hatch during runoff but are nearly impossible to fish in the muddy water. Some diehards pound big stonefly nymphs along the banks but fishing isn't what you could call reliable. Sometimes the water has cleared in the upper sections of the river towards the end of the salmonfly hatch, and anglers ready to head there at the drop of a hat can get in on the action.

Hatches throughout the summer are consistent and varied. There are good mayfly, caddis and stonefly hatches all season long, and anglers should be prepared for just about anything. Don't forget a box of hoppers if you happen here during the late summer and early fall. Hopper fishing on the Blackfoot is about as good as it gets.

If you plan on floating the Blackfoot, do your homework first. While sections can be negotiated without too many problems, there are other sections that only experienced rafters should attempt. Many rapids are scattered along the river, and depending on water flow, some can be pretty hairy. Ask, and scout to be safe.

As previously mentioned, access on the Blackfoot is very good via Highway 200. Several camping areas are located along the way, and motels can be found in Missoula and Lincoln.

Little Blackfoot River

Although not as well known as the Blackfoot River, the Little Blackfoot is a river worthy of attention in its own right. The Little Blackfoot heads in the Helena National Forest, and flows into the Clark Fork River near Garrison, a distance of 39 miles.

The lower sections of the river are severely dewatered by ranchers, access is poor, but there are some nice-sized brown trout found here. Access is mostly from highway bridges—just remember to stay below the high water mark and you will be within the law.

Brown trout are found throughout most of the river, including some large spawners traveling upstream from the Clark Fork. In the extreme upper reaches cutthroat and brook trout are predominant. Access here is via dirt road from Elliston.

The Little Blackfoot hatches are pretty typical for a western river. Winter sees midges; pre-runoff you have *Baetis*, and the start of the caddis hatches. After runoff and throughout the summer you have a variety of caddis, mayflies and stoneflies. Hoppers and other terrestrials are important during the summer as well.

Anaconda Settling Ponds

If you are headed for Montana to soak in the "Big Sky" beauty, and you only have a couple days to do it, you might want to pass on the Anaconda Settling Ponds—because they are ugly. But if you have reveled in the beauty long enough and simply want to catch a "hog," this just might be the place for a few hours of hunting.

Prior to the building of the settling ponds, toxic runoff from mining waste turned the upper Clark Fork Red. Nothing lived here, not even algae. The series of shallow ponds were built to contain and treat the water of Silver Bow Creek, the chief tributary of the upper Clark Fork. There are still plenty of toxins that make it into the upper Clark Fork resulting in fish kills from time to time. But at least the water spilling from the last pond, the official start of the Clark Fork River, is now clean enough to support trout, mostly browns, which can tolerate more pollutants than the other trout species.

Surprisingly, in the ponds themselves, trout grow to enormous dimensions. Rainbows and browns of over 10 pounds are taken here often enough that the ponds have a regular following of anglers. The toxic sediment gets covered with thick aquatic vegetation, which in turn host insects, snails, scuds and monster leeches. The trout have plenty to eat, in fact, so much, that it is not an easy task getting one of these hogs to take an artificial fly. Still, it can be done, but requires patience and determination.

Snail and scud patterns are probably the most consistent flies in the settling ponds. The most effective method of making contact with a fish is to stalk them. Sneaking up to the shoreline and viewing with polarized glasses will let you spot foraging fish. Placing a fly in the trout's path of travel simply increases your odds.

Another method is to use large leech patterns. Sizes 4 or

Opposite page: Blackfoot River.
Below: A hefty rainbow.

Brown trout caught while tubing a Montana lake.

Blackfeet Reservation Lakes

Just to the east of Glacier National Park, the Blackfeet Indian Reservation covers a considerable chunk of windswept prairie. This can be a desolate place. During spring and fall (the best fishing seasons) driving rain, hail, sleet, and snow can pound this part of Montana. Combined with the seemingly incessant winds, well, you get the picture. Still, the reservation has plenty to offer the fly angler.

Scattered around the reservation are lakes, many of which have been carefully managed to produce trout—some of gargantuan proportions. There is probably no other place in Montana where anglers can travel, realistically expecting to catch trout of five- pounds or better.

The town of Browning is located on the reservation. U.S Highway 2 or 89 will get you there. Tribal fishing licenses can be bought in Browning or in East Glacier and, when you buy your license you are given a map with directions to all the open waters on the reservation, along with a list of rules and regulations.

It is important to read the regulations carefully. A couple things to note: on the reservation, non-tribal members must be off the water by sunset. Not dusk—not dark— but sunset! I know, from personal experience. Likewise, you are not permitted to fish before sunrise. And when buying your license, keep in mind that it costs extra to fish out of a float tube or boat.

even size 2 Bunny Leeches will work. Remembering that you are here after large fish, size your tippet and rod accordingly.

For those who enjoy such a thing, night fishing the ponds is probably the best time, as big fish are on the take, and loose many of their daytime inhibitions. Large leech patterns are the standard for night fishing.

To reach the settling ponds take the Warm Springs exit off Interstate 90, and turn left. Follow the dirt access road to the ugly piles that contain the lakes.

Steve Probasco with a respectable Blackfeet Reservation rainbow.

When fishing the Blackfeet Reservation, regulations state that you are to be off the water by sunset. This photo cost me $25.

You will find all the basic hatches of stillwater insects in the reservation lakes. In addition, many of the lakes have good sculpin populations, which warrants including a few Muddler Minnows in your arsenal of gear. Leeches and scuds are prevalent also, as is the Callibaetis mayfly.

A good selection of fly patterns for the reservation lakes would include the Gold Ribbed Hare's Ear Nymph, PMDs, black and olive Woolly Buggers, Muddler Minnow, Zonkers, dragonfly and damselfly nymphs, various leeches, and scud patterns.

There is limited camping available on the reservation, consequently most visiting anglers stay in Browning, East Glacier, Cut Bank or St. Mary. It is wise to obey all regulations and respect private property. For current regulations you can contact the Blackfeet Nation at (406) 338-7207.

Guided fishing is available, and is a great way to learn the water. A guide that I have fished with and can highly recommend is Joe Kipp, of Morning Star Outfitters in Browning (406) 338-2785. Fishing with a guide will also put you on some waters that are not open to the general public.

There are many quality lakes on the reservation. Following is a list of the most popular fisheries, but this list certainly doesn't include all the angling possibilities found on the reservation. The map you get when you buy your license will reveal a host of other opportunities.

Duck Lake

Duck is one of the reservations most popular lakes. Surrounded by houses, the setting seems less remote than the other reservation lakes. However, the population of large trout makes up for the view. It is believed that Duck Lake hosts more large fish than any other reservation lake.

Rainbow and brown trout to 10 pounds are taken in Duck Lake. In addition, bull trout have been planted to help keep the lake's sucker population in check. Anglers both tube and cast from shore in this prolific lake.

Like most lakes, Duck is either off or on. When it's on, you are in for a treat. Woolly Buggers cast from the shore, or from a float tube will produce unbelievable results. When it's off though, you might as well move on to another lake. The best fishing is in the spring and fall.

Mission Lake

Mission Lake sits in a high valley and is somewhat sheltered from the wind, at least compared to some of the other reservation lakes. This lake is very rich in aquatic life, from its weedy bottom, to its insects, to its rainbow trout that thrive in both numbers and size.

Damselflies are a major food item for Mission's trout, and consequently, damsel nymphs seductively worked just under the surface get a lot of attention. Midges, Callibaetis mayflies, leeches—all the standard lake foods are abundant here.

Mitten Lake

Mitten is another rich, high valley lake that produces rainbow trout in both size and numbers. Extensive weed beds make Mitten a good bet for consistent summer hatches.

Kipp Lake

Located just to the northeast of Browning, Kipp Lake sees plenty of pressure. It does, however, continue to be one of the best lakes on the reservation for size and numbers of rainbow trout.

Kipp Lake sits in a hollow in the windswept prairie, and although not the prettiest lake in the state, it is incredibly rich. The weedy bottom and aquatic life ensures plenty of trout food. Fish it slowly with intermediate lines to stay out of the weeds.

Four Horn Lake

Four Horn Lake is large (750 acres) and like many of the larger reservation lakes the wind howls here with a vengeance. Large rainbow and brown trout are the attraction here. Sinking lines and large streamers account for the biggest fish.

Dog Gun Lake

Dog Gun is a brook trout lake located on the western edge of the reservation close to East Glacier. This is a shallow lake best fished with streamers on an intermediate or floating line for brookies up to five pounds.

Georgetown Lake

With its rich aquatic life; extensive weed beds, insects and fish population, it is amazing that Georgetown Lake is a mountain lake—6,000 feet in elevation. This is a major destination fishery for stillwater anglers. Georgetown hosts three strains of rainbow trout, brook trout, and Kokanee salmon.

The three strains of rainbow trout include; Arlee, Eagle Lake, and Kamloops. Rainbows up to 7 pounds are not uncommon here, and brook trout in the 3- to 5-pound range

Fishing a secluded Blackfeet Reservation lake.

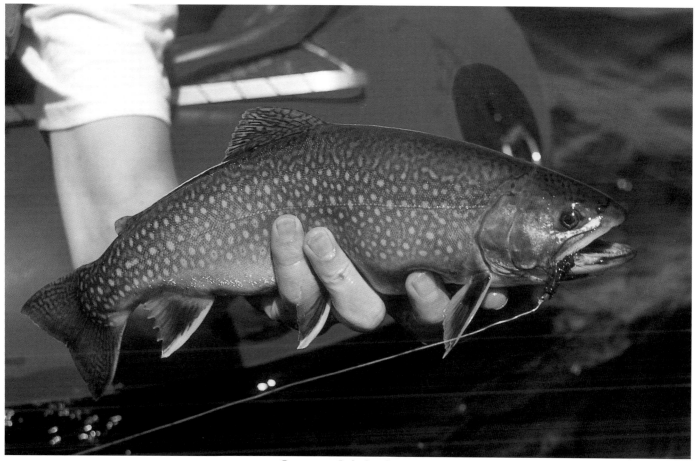

Georgetown Lake brook trout.

come from Georgetown's fertile waters. With fish like these, it's easy to see why this lake is so popular among fly anglers.

The Kokanee salmon have been a thorn-in-the-side to fly-fishers. They are very effective predators, and interfere with the rainbows in search of food. It was the intention of the introduction of the Kamloops and Eagle Lake strain of rainbows to control the Kokanee by eating their young. This hasn't worked out quite as planned, but today, generous and regular plants of rainbows are keeping the populations of Kokanee in check.

Georgetown Lake is fairly shallow, with a maximum depth of less than 40 feet. Most of the lake is much less than that, and aquatic weed growth can interfere with fishing during the summer months. When the vegetation is bad, one of the best places to fish is a fairly open area just out from the pump house located on the east side of the lake. There is a public boat launch close by.

Float tubes, small personal boats, and motorized crafts are all found on this lake. However, due to the shallow, weedy bays where much of the fishing takes place, float tubes and small personal boats are favored for fly-fishing anglers.

Probably the best fishing on this lake occurs during the damselfly migration, from mid-June through the first part of July. When the damsel nymphs swim towards shore they create a feeding frenzy that local fly-fishers are sure to be on top of. Any olive damselfly nymph imitation (as long as it has a

marabou tail) in size 12 or 10 will work well. Intermediate and sinking-tip lines are perfect for this type of fishing.

There is a good Callibaetis hatch on the lake in the bays, and a size 14 Parachute Adams is hard to beat. There is also a hatch of traveling sedges (caddis) that come off in late July on into August. These big (size 8) caddis swim to shore leaving a wake behind them. Adult patterns fished to mimic the naturals will result in some explosive strikes.

For those targeting the brook trout, Woolly Buggers,

Georgetown Lake Lodge.

Zonkers, and other streamers are your best bet. They can be taken all season, but perhaps the best time would be during fall along the gravel shorelines. Egg-Sucking Buggers are hard to beat.

When traveling to Georgetown Lake, keep in mind that at 6,000 feet you can expect any kind of weather most of the season. Summer snowstorms and thunderstorms can roll through theses mountains anytime— so be prepared.

Camping is available at several improved and unimproved areas around the lake. There is a lodge located on the south end with rooms, a bar and restaurant.

To reach Georgetown Lake take Highway 1 south from Drummond, or west from Anaconda. The highway skirts the northeastern shore of the lake, and a lesser road travels around the lake providing good access.

Flint Creek

Flint Creek tumbles from the dam that contains Georgetown Lake, just south of Philipsburg. Winding through a steep canyon, Flint Creek eventually finds its way to the Philipsburg Valley floor. It is roughly paralleled by Highway 1 all the way to its confluence with the Clark Fork, near Drummond.

It would be hard to find a prettier, fishier, valley stream than Flint Creek. The problem is, most of the land through which it flows is private. That's not to say you can't fish, but you better be on your best of manners and ask permission. Gaining access through private property is the only real way to fish this creek, except for access at bridges and at the mouth. Still, you must obey the stream access law.

If you enjoy crashing through streamside willows, swatting mosquitoes, loosing flies in the brush and sunken jungles associated with valley streams—you will love Flint Creek. Frustrating? Yes. But small streams have a way of getting under your skin.

In return for their frustrations and perseverance to gain access, anglers will be rewarded with an intimate little stream that harbors brown trout the size you might expect to come from a much larger river. But keep in mind—they don't come easy.

Flint Creek presents with undercut banks, deep holes, and a snaky, willow-lined course. The largest fish (big browns) will be tucked under banks and in the tangle of sunken brush and root wads. This makes for tough fishing. Big streamers will coax a strike, but often ends with a snapped tippet. One of the best (and most fun) times to take the larger browns is during

Lightning storm over Georgetown Lake.

hopper season. The big guys will leave their lair to smack a big, juicy grasshopper. Any high-floating hopper pattern should do the trick.

Besides the browns found in Flint Creek, smaller cutthroat, rainbow and brook trout, as well as whitefish are available.

An area worthwhile during fall is the lower mile or so of Flint Creek, and the area around its confluence with the Clark Fork. Big browns from the river spawn in this tributary. It can be a scary affair!

Highway 1 and Flint Creek is reached from Interstate 90 at the Drummond exit, and from upper Rock Creek by following Rock Creek Road to Highway 38 and turning east.

Flathead Indian Reservation

Over a million acres of land containing rivers, streams, lowland lakes, ponds, reservoirs and alpine lakes fall within the boundaries of the Flathead Indian Reservation. Cutthroat, rainbow, brown and bull trout, as well as northern pike and largemouth bass inhabit their waters.

The Flathead Reservation is located south of Glacier National Park. The southern half of Flathead Lake is located on the reservation, as is the lower Flathead River and many other waters to the west and south. The eastern boundary of the reservation extends into the Mission Mountains where many alpine lakes are found. One could spend an entire fishing season exploring the waters of the reservation and still not do it all. Remember that a tribal permit is required to fish here.

Flathead Reservation fisheries management is working very well. Through a cooperative effort between the Salish and Kootenai tribes, the natural resources of the reservation are of high priority (what a novel idea) and special consideration is given the fisheries.

Some of the waters located on the Flathead Reservation have previously been covered in this book. However, there are many more worth exploring. For further information, contact the Flathead Indian Reservation, Tribal Fish, Wildlife, Recreation and Conservation Division, P.O. Box 278, Pablo, MT 59855, (406) 675-2700.

Glacier National Park

Glacier National Park doesn't usually come to mind for anglers traveling to Montana or warrant too long of a drive by natives—just for the fishing. If it's size and variety you are after, you probably won't be happy in Glacier. And if driving

Driving the country roads can often lead you to special places.

at a snail's pace behind tourists rubs you the wrong way, you best head elsewhere.

But Glacier Park does have plenty to offer those willing to hike for their fish, brave the mosquitoes and grizzly bears and settle for trout on the small size (comparably speaking, of course).

For those who enjoy alpine fishing in a remote setting, Glacier National Park just might be your ultimate fishing destination. This is classic alpine angling, with unparalleled scenery. As for fish, those who look hard enough can find Westslope and Yellowstone cutthroat, rainbow, brook, lake and bull trout; grayling are found in some waters.

The key to getting into the best fishing in the Park is to cover some ground. It doesn't take long to get "remote" here, but backcountry travelers need to keep in mind that this is grizzly bear country. Park bears have been around plenty of people and some are no longer wary. Whenever off the beaten path, make plenty of noise and be careful of how you store your food.

As with most alpine fishing, remote trout are not usually particular about the flies they attack—if it looks like food it gets smacked. Attractor dries like the Humpy and Royal Wulff work well, as will time-proven standards like the Adams and Elk Hair Caddis for dries, and the Hare's Ear Nymph, Pheasant Tail and Tellico for nymphs. A 3- to 5-weight rod is adequate for most fishing situations you will encounter.

The Continental Divide splits Glacier into western and eastern drainages. The western drainage is wetter, and streams get migratory runs of cutthroat and bull trout. The eastern drainage is much drier, and streams contain mostly small brookies. The alpine lakes are the real attraction, with a broader variety of species, and the angling is far superior to that found in the streams.

There are a plethora of waters to fish in Glacier National Park. Some of the notable streams and lakes draining west include; Camas Lake and Creek (Yellowstone cutthroat), Harrison Lake and Creek (native cutthroat and bull trout), Ellen Wilson Lake (brook trout), Hidden Lake (Yellowstone cutthroat), Lincoln Lake (native cutthroat) and McDonald Lake (native cutthroat).

Some of the most popular waters in the eastern drainage include; Gunsight Lake (rainbows), Ptarmigan Lake (brook trout), Upper Two Medicine Lake (brook and rainbow trout) and Red Eagle Lake (rainbow and cutthroat trout).

In addition, the northern part of the Park, which is even more remote and grizzly infested, hosts some great and unique fishing. Some of the more noted waters include; Belly River (rainbow and brook trout, grayling), Glenn's Lake (cutthroat, brook and lake trout), Kootenai Lakes (brook trout) and Frances Lake (rainbows).

Whenever traveling into the alpine regions of Glacier, call the Park Service first. Certain areas may not be open because of snow, winterkill or too many bears. Glacier National Park (406) 888-5441.

Spring wildflowers.

The Central Fishing District of Montana includes all waters east of the Continental Divide, to a boundary definition in the Montana Fish Wildlife & Parks, Fishing Regulations Pamphlet that you just have to read to picture. Let's just say that Central Montana the best part of the state in which to fish. It contains several of the state's most famous rivers. To many anglers, this is Montana.

Central Montana includes such fabled waters as the Big Hole, Beaverhead, Missouri, Madison, Gallatin, Yellowstone and a host of others. The number of quality rivers, streams, spring creeks, lakes and reservoirs found here is mind boggling.

Central Montana hosts many mountain ranges, where many headwaters are born. Many of the famous rivers of Central Montana join with other famous streams to form yet other famous rivers. For example; the Madison joins the Gallatin and Jefferson rivers to form the Missouri River. The Big Hole, Beaverhead and Ruby rivers join to form the Jefferson river. Get the picture?

The trout found in the Central District are as varied as the water in which they are found. Cutthroat, golden, rainbow and brook trout can be found in mountain streams and lakes. Rainbow and brown trout, some of gargantuan proportions, can be found in many of the lower rivers and lakes. And grayling can be found in a

Fishing the upper Big Hole River.

few places, most noted are those found in the upper Big Hole River; Montana's last viable population of fluvial (river-dwelling) grayling.

Although this part of Montana hosts trout of staggering size and numbers, they are not always easy to take. It's one thing to pick trout off one after another during a salmonfly hatch, and quite another to get frustrated, then skunked, as picky fish snub your perfectly presented Trico. It can happen. Humble pie has been served to some awfully good anglers in Montana.

One would think that with all the friends the famous rivers have their security and protection would be an assured thing. Not so. The Central Fishing District faces the same problems as the rest of Montana. The land comes first. Consumptive interests, in these parts, mostly in the form of overgrazing and de-watering from overzealous irrigation, take their toll. Drought years especially remind us of this. All of Montana needs friends—watchdogs to keep the bad guys in check!

Big Hole River

The Big Hole, like most rivers, is a river of many faces, but perhaps has a few more faces than most rivers. It begins as the outlet of Skinner Lake in the Beaverhead Mountains south of Jackson, Montana. It rushes down to the valley below and is joined by the North Fork of the Big Hole downstream from Wisdom. To this point, the Big Hole

Overleaf: Madison Mountain Range and rangeland near the Madison River.

Big Hole River brown that fell for a Girdle Bug.

contains only small brookies, cutthroat and grayling. From the point where the forks join, on downstream, the Big Hole becomes a fascinating river.

From Wisdom downstream for several miles, the Big Hole braids through farmland. Brushy banks of willow line the

Salmonfly imitations.

river here (really just a stream) and it harbors mostly small brook trout and grayling, but as you get farther downstream, rainbows and a few browns start to appear. Once the river reaches Squaw Creek, it becomes larger, with grassy banks, and is an easy river to fly-fish.

Downstream, trout populations continue to increase and when the river reaches Wise River there is a major change. Just upstream from here, springs enter the Big Hole, providing ideal conditions for aquatic life. Trout populations jump, mostly rainbows, but there is also a healthy population of browns. Moving on downstream the river flows through a canyon. Highway 43 parallels the river here, providing great access to the wading angler. Pocket water, riffles, pools and tailouts provide water suited to all sorts of tactics. Dry flies, nymphs and streamers all have their place here and there are some big trout living in this water.

From Divide, the river flows away from the road and is mostly fished by the floating angler. This is the fishiest section of the entire river (electrofishing estimates up to 3,500 fish per mile), with rainbow and brown trout found in equal

Opposite page: The Big Hole River near Divide during fall.

A fall brown from the lower Big Hole.

numbers. Floaters using big nymphs and streamers take fish to 5 pounds or more here. Salmon Fly (Melrose Bridge) is usually the exit point for this float.

The Melrose Bridge downstream to Glen offers much quieter water, with plenty of fish (mostly browns) available from grassy, undercut banks and around other structure. Big streamers pitched to the bank are responsible for plenty of sore mouths. Brown trout of over 20 inches are commonly

taken, with a true monster landed now and then.

During fall, from Glen to the Big Hole's confluence with the Beaverhead River you can find some awfully big brown trout—but you have to work for them. Large streamers punched to the banks and stripped back rapidly will often produce browns of incredible proportions. Not a lot of them but some fish to write home about!

Hatches on the Big Hole are reliable and predictable. It all begins in March with the *Baetis* making an appearance. The first really big hatch is that of the Grannom caddis, commonly known as the "Mothers' Day Hatch," because it happens around that time. This is a heavy hatch that lasts for several days. A size 14 Elk Hair Caddis with a dark olive body will do the trick.

The big salmonfly hatch hits the Big Hole the first week in June. Anglers materialize from all over to partake in this event. The reason, besides being a great hatch, is that the Big Hole seldom turns chocolate during runoff like many other Montana rivers. The river can blow and become unfishable, but it is less common here.

As the summer progresses a variety of hatches appear. Green drakes, brown drakes, PMDs, more stoneflies and caddis—the Big Hole is a dry-fly angler's dream. Tricos and hoppers are important during the heat of summer and black flying

Angling the Big Hole below Brown's Bridge during the fall.

Spring fishing the middle section of the Big Hole River.

early in the morning and then again late into the evening, even into the darkness. Big streamers will nail their share of big fish even during the summer lull.

The entire Big Hole River is floatable. There are several public access points scattered along its length. Some of the popular floats include; Sportsman Park to Jerry Creek, Jerry Creek to Maiden Rock, Maiden Rock to Salmon Fly, and Salmon Fly to Brown's Bridge. The most challenging section for floaters is the stretch between Maiden Rock and Melrose. Some maneuvering and common sense is needed here.

Big Hole grayling are Montana's last viable population of fluvial (river-dwelling) grayling. These fish only survive in clean water. Rightly protected, these fish must be released unharmed, as with the cutthroat trout. But then all the trout you catch in the Big Hole should be released unharmed, right? Right!

As good as the Big Hole River is, still it suffers from the same problems that face many Montana rivers, especially during drought years; de-watering by irrigation and careless grazing practices. During the summer of 1994 when I was doing research for my book, River Journal, Big Hole, the river was closed to angling because of low levels and high water temperatures. Driving along the river you could still see ineffective and wasteful irrigation practices. In the upper river you could also see cattle standing in the middle of the river. Go figure!

The Big Hole can be reached by taking Interstate 15 south from Butte and exiting at Divide, Melrose or Glen. Highway 43 follows the Big Hole to its upper reaches and connects with Highway 273 to Anaconda, then continues west over the mountains to Missoula. Several campgrounds are located along the river. Food, lodging and gas are available but limited in Jackson, Wisdom and Melrose. All services are available in Dillon. There are several fly shops and outfitters located along the upper Big Hole.

ants cause a commotion in September. This river fishes well for most of the season but does have a mid summer slow-down. During August sometimes the best tactic is to fish very

Average Big Hole grayling.

Choose your shortcuts carefully!

Beaverhead River

The Lewis and Clark expedition camped in a valley near the confluence of Red Rock River and Horse Prairie Creek in 1805. Camp Fortunate, as it was called, was the jump-off point for their horse exploration of the Bitterroot Country. This spot also served as a cache for some of their equipment. This would have been the beginning of what is now the Beaverhead River. An entry in their diary tells of numerous trout taken from this stream. In 1964, the stream was dammed, flooding the valley. The Beaverhead's official beginning is now the outflow of Clark Canyon Dam. It flows nearly 80 miles before its confluence with the Big Hole River. Although much has changed since Lewis and Clark explored these parts, one thing remains in the Beaverhead—its incredible trout fishing.

Above: Tim Mondale with a Beaverhead rainbow.
Right: The beginning of the Beaverhead from Clark Canyon Dam.

I read at one time that every 10 feet the Beaverhead hosts a trout of 20 inches. I don't know if this is true or not, but I do know that the Beaverhead kicks out some awfully large fish, both rainbows and browns—especially browns. Trout well over 10 pounds are hooked in this little stream.

From Clark Canyon Dam downstream to Barrett's Diversion Dam (the heaviest-fished section) there are several public access points. The first is right below the dam. Then you come to High Bridge (1.2 miles), Hanneberry Bridge (7 miles), Pipe Organ Bridge (9 miles) and Barrett's at 12 miles. A frontage road parallels the river from Clark Canyon

Reservoir for the first few miles, and exits off Interstate 15 provide access at the bridges.

Barrett's Diversion Dam steals half of the Beaverhead's water during the irrigation season. Consequently, the size and numbers of fish are down below this point. However, wading is much easier and anglers pounding the banks catch a fair number of browns.

Beyond doubt, the best way to fish the Beaverhead is to float it. This is especially true during heavy snow-pack, high-water years when wading the swift current is just too difficult. Combined with the willows that line the banks, the wading angler can have it tough. This all changes during fall, once the irrigation flow is shut down. At this time, the Beaverhead can be easily waded from all the public access points.

Even though the Beaverhead hosts upwards of 2,000 fish per mile, getting them to take a fly should not be taken for granted. Beaverhead trout can be as tough as any trout—anywhere!

Rods in the 6- to 7-weight range are the best here. Even though the Beaverhead looks like a small-rod stream, keep in mind the size of the trout, the current and the aquatic jungle on the bottom. Use as heavy a leader as you can get away with. A 3X will often spook the fish, but is also often the minimum for consistently landing one of the larger fish. It's a gamble, any way you look at it.

Although there are some heavy and reliable hatches that can briefly turn the Beaverhead into a top-water frenzy, this river is mostly thought of as a nymphing stream.

Most of the time the fish will be down in the weeds or tucked into the willows. Floating along, bottom-bouncing a weighted Hare's Ear Nymph, Pheasant Tail Nymph, Prince Nymph or Midge pupa will account for plenty of hook-ups. Landing a fish once hooked is another matter. The swift current and bottom mosses ensure you work for your fish.

When hatches are present you can expect to find PMDs, *Baetis*, various small stoneflies, midges, caddis and perhaps the most interesting hatch, the cranefly. Most of the action will be on cranefly larvae that get washed into the stream after rainstorms, but when adults are present, trout go nuts for them. Skating flies like the Ginger Spider, and specific adult cranefly imitations work well.

Fall fishing on the Beaverhead.

Another good method on the Beaverhead is streamer fishing, especially during the fall. Large (size 4 or 2) Muddlers, Zonkers and Buggers take their share of large browns. Streamer fishing is also very effective during late evening and into the darkness of night. A floating line, hefty rod, 0X tippet and nerves of steel are all it takes.

All amenities are found in the town of Dillon, about 10 miles north of Clark Canyon Dam, including fly shops and guide services.

Grasshopper Creek

In 1862 gold was found on Grasshopper Creek and the mining camp of Bannack was established. This Beaverhead tributary is not large but is certainly worthy of mention. With its beginning in the Pioneer Mountains northwest of Dillon, Grasshopper Creek empties into the Beaverhead about 14 miles downstream from Clark Canyon Dam.

Its headwaters are located near Elkhorn Hot Springs. In this area you can expect to find mostly small brookies. The best fishing is found downstream around the ghost town of Bannack. Lots of private property is found here, but access can be had. Rainbows and browns to 20 inches are around for those willing to hunt them.

The upper reaches of Rattlesnake Creek winds through undercut banks, hay and sage fields, and eventually through a canyon before merging with the Beaverhead. After a big rain, this creek turns chocolate and is unfishable. It actually muddies the entire Beaverhead below its entrance.

BWOs, PMDs, caddisflies—all the basics can be found here. Hopper patterns are especially productive during the late summer. Close to the Beaverhead, streamers often produce some big surprises during the fall.

Access is from Highway 278. Camping is available at Elkhorn Hot Springs and near Bannack.

An approaching storm over the Beaverhead north of Dillon.

Poindexter Slough

Poindexter Slough is a spring creek not unlike many western spring creeks, with one major exception—it's not located on private property and you don't have to pay a fee to fish there. It's a classic spring creek; prolific hatches, plenty of fish, year round angling and, at times, painfully difficult.

Access to Poindexter Slough is easy, it's located off Interstate 15, just south of Dillon. This makes Poindexter a great side-trip when fishing the Beaverhead, Big Hole or Clark Canyon Reservoir.

In typical spring-creek fashion, hatches are abundant, timely and generally small in size. Also in typical spring-creek fashion, even the largest of trout will tune-in on whatever hatch is on the menu. Small flies, long leaders (12 to 16 feet) and light tippets (6X to 8X) make for some interesting fishing, especially when one of the big boys takes your fly.

Hatches during the winter are limited to small midges and as the season rolls along, various mayflies and caddisflies make their appearance. As with most spring-creek fishing, the naturals are on the small side. Anglers should arrive with an assortment of small dries and nymphs (sizes 16 to 22), including patterns such as the Parachute Adams, Griffith's Gnat, PMD, *Baetis*, Serendipity, Pheasant Tail, Hare's Ear and Brassie.

Clark Canyon Reservoir

Clark Canyon Reservoir is perhaps the best public stillwater fishery in the state of Montana. Located just 20 miles south of Dillon, this 6,000-acre reservoir kicks out enough 5- to 10-pound rainbows and browns to get any stillwater angler excited. Access is good and, most of the time, the angling is too.

In 1964 Clark Canyon Dam was built to contain the waters of the Red Rock River and Horse Prairie Creek for irrigation purposes. Clark Canyon Reservoir is the result. The Beaverhead River flows from the base of the dam.

Fishing gets underway as soon as the ice breaks in the spring, usually in late March. At this time, trout can be found cruising the shorelines in the open water. When the ice completely disappears, the shallow, south end of the lake is the place to be. The prolific weed beds found here host an amazing number of insects which, of course, attract the trout.

As soon as there is open water, and the water temperature warms a bit, Chironomids hatch on the reservoir in a big way. Clouds of these midges swarm about, at times making it hard to breathe without sucking a few bugs into your throat. A size 12 pupal pattern in dark olive or black is killer when fished in the surface film.

In June, the Callibaetis mayfly hatch can be intense, Hare's Ear Nymphs for the emergers and Parachute Adams

Charlie Busteed nets a hefty Clark Canyon Reservoir rainbow.

Tubers working the shallows on the south end of Clark Canyon Reservoir.

in size 12 are hard to beat. In July, the damselfly emergence is phenomenal. Marabou patterns with lots of wiggle will produce plenty of action. Leech patterns will work any time and result in a healthy share of the larger fish.

On the south end, an intermediate sinking line or a sinking-tip line is the most practical. Keep in mind that this is shallow water. In fact, by fall many of the best fishing spots found during the spring are high-and-dry due to the irrigation drawdown.

There is an old road that leads into the lake (Red Rock Access) on the southeastern corner of the reservoir. This is a great place to launch a boat or tube when planning to fish the

mouth of the Red Rock River. There are plenty of sunken willows here but the payoff for a few lost flies are the big fish that congregate here, especially during spring and fall.

Although the south end of the lake is the best for float tubing, trout can be found cruising along just about any shoreline, and during the heat of summer they can also be

Tom Schwiesow with an average Clark Canyon Reservoir rainbow.

Chironomid hatches are heavy during spring on Clark Canyon Reservoir.

found in numbers along the drop-offs near the dam and on the south side of the big island.

Rods in the 5- to 7-weight range and intermediate to full-sinking lines all have a place here. The trout are not too fussy, and except for the top-water flies, you can usually get away with using 3X tippet. Although you could wade and cast from shore, a float tube or a boat will certainly put you over more fish.

The biggest problem with fishing Clark Canyon Reservoir is the wind—it can howl here! Keep this in mind when making a trip or venturing onto this water. If it's a problem, there are always things close-by to do; the Beaverhead, Poindexter Slough, Red Rock River and the Big Hole.

There are two boat launches on the reservoir; one located just south of Clark Canyon Dam and another on the west side shore. Camping is available on the north, south and east sides of the lake. A perimeter road circles the lake. All services are located in Dillon, 20 miles to the north.

Red Rock River

The Red Rock River comes to life in the Centennial Mountains, near the Idaho border. During its course, the river flows through Red Rock Lakes (closed to fishing) and then on to Lima Reservoir, eventually emptying into Clark Canyon Reservoir.

If it weren't for the fact that most of the best water on the Red Rock flows through private property, this would be one of the most popular rivers in the state. Unfortunately, public access is very limited. The best shot at gaining access (other than knowing a landowner or paying a fee) is that stretch of water near where the river dumps into Clark Canyon Reservoir, or on the upper reaches.

The upper reaches of the river can be excellent for cutthroat, as well as grayling—one of the few rivers left in the lower 48 to host these fish. The upper Red Rock is a smallish stream, perfectly suited to wading. Nearly any high-floating dry fly will produce here.

The river below Lima Reservoir, and all the way to Clark Canyon Reservoir is the stretch that gets all the hype. The river here winds through agricultural land, with overhanging banks, willows and trout eager to smack a dry fly. A variety of caddis and mayflies can be found here but hoppers steal the show during the summer and early fall. Rainbow and brown trout (some to several pounds) dominate. As I mentioned, access is the big problem, and a certain bit of creativity is needed to fish here .

The immediate area around where the river spills into Clark Canyon Reservoir is on Bureau of Reclamation land, and provides some access. This small section of the lower river is especially good during early spring for pre-spawn rainbows heading up from the lake, and again during fall for those migrating browns. Timing is everything!

Jefferson River, near Twin Bridges.

German brown trout.

To reach the upper Red Rock River, exit Interstate 15 at Monida (Exit 0) and follow the dirt road leading to Red Rock Pass. Follow the access signs to the river. The lower river can be accessed by taking Exit 37 off Interstate 15 to the south side of Clark Canyon Reservoir. The river enters on the southeast corner of the reservoir.

Jefferson River

When Lewis and Clark passed through the area in 1805, they named the Jefferson River after the country's president at that time, Thomas Jefferson. With its beginning where the Beaverhead and Big Hole rivers meet, just north of Twin Bridges, the Jefferson travels through agricultural and cattle country, along the Tabacco Root Mountains, joining the Madison and Galatin rivers to form the Missouri, some 60 miles distant.

The Jefferson is a big, slow river. It is not easily waded, and is best fished by floating. It is not known as a major Montana trout destination, but it is known by a few as the place to be for large brown trout during the fall. The Jefferson has a loyal following of trophy hunters.

Runoff begins in May and continues through June. Irrigation then begins and continues through September. What this really means is that the Jefferson isn't clear until all this is over. Fish can be taken all season but don't expect crystal-clear water.

For oarsmen of moderate skill, the Jefferson presents few problems. In fact, if there is a wind blowing upstream you sometimes need to row downstream just to make progress. Even though the floating is relatively easy, one still needs to be on the lookout for the occasional logjam and water diversion.

Most of the angling action takes place on the upper river between Twin Bridges and Cardwell. This is also the most popular float. This section is faster paced than the rest of the river and also has more trout per mile. Rainbows and browns are both found, with the browns considerably outnumbering the rainbows. The river is braided here in places making for good food and habitat. Streamers and nymphs are favored, especially during fall.

The canyon stretch, below Cardwell, is much deeper and slower. Access is from Highway 10, and a campground. Fishing can be good at times, as the canyon walls provide daily shade on the water.

The lower section, from the canyon to Headwaters State Park, is slow, braided, lined with cottonwoods, difficult to float in low-water years and, at times, holds some monster brown trout. Those who put in their dues often catch a fish to write home about—for sure!

If you venture to the Jefferson in search of the run-of-the-mill rainbow or brown during the summer months, bring the usual flies—those that match the hatches. But, if you come in the fall, in search of the behemoth browns, come prepared with big streamers; Muddlers, Spuddlers, Zonkers, Matukas and the like. Size 1 is not too large.

Ruby River

Natives called it the Passamari, and Captain William Clark renamed it the Philanthropy. Later still, it was known as the Stinkingwater and today it is known as the Ruby—named for the red garnets found in the river's bottom gravel. Whatever you want to call it, this is a great little trout stream. The Ruby's headwaters are in the Snowcrest Range. The river flows for roughly 65 miles before emptying into the Beaverhead River, near Twin Bridges.

For many years the Ruby was off limits to anglers who didn't have an "in" with a local landowner hadn't mastered the fine art of sneaking or were unwilling to pay a stiff access fee. Recently, the Montana Department of Fish, Wildlife and Parks has leased a few access sites where anglers can "legally" slip into the river. Still, there is a sour taste in many locals' mouths over this development.

The Ruby is a small, meandering stream with willow-lined banks. It is the perfect stream for a lazy summer's wade, casting hoppers along the undercut banks. Brown trout are predominant, and a large fish from this river will be an 18- or 20-incher.

The upper river, above Ruby Reservoir, hosts rainbow, cutthroat, a few browns and grayling. Access is through Forest Service land. The trout here will run smaller than in the lower river, but they are willing to take a variety of dry flies.

The Ruby is reached from Highway 287 out of Twin Bridges. Follow Upper Ruby Road above the reservoir for upper river access.

Missouri River

The Missouri River begins with the union of the Madison, Gallatin and Jefferson rivers at Three Forks, Montana. Although a large, lengthy and somewhat intimidating river, the 35-mile stretch from Holter Dam to Cascade is one of the best trout streams in the state.

Below Holter Dam the Missouri resembles a gigantic spring creek, with dense weed beds, prolific hatches and a generous population of rainbow and brown trout reaching 20 inches or more. In fact, trout to 10 pounds are caught here each year, but catching these fish often requires spring-creek stealth and tactics by the angler. Missouri fish are no pushover.

Even though it is the stretch of river below Holter Dam that gets the attention of most fly anglers, the 3-mile section of river between Hauser Dam to Holter Lake kicks out some

Floating the Missouri River below Craig.

nice fish to ambitious anglers (you have to hoof it), especially large brown trout near the outlet of the dam. Heavy heads and weighted streamers are needed to get down here. Downstream a ways you will find water suitable for dry-fly or nymph fishing, although trout populations are not as heavy as in the river below Holter Dam.

The Missouri River is a year-round fishery, limited in the winter only by extended cold-weather periods. During the cold-weather months, midges can hatch in hoards, creating exceptional winter angling. Tiny dry flies are the rule; Griffith's Gnats, Adams and specific midge imitations are effective, as are midge pupas under the surface.

By April, *Baetis* begin their appearance, and by May they are the major hatch. The *Baetis* are overlapped by caddis, which also begin in late May, and become the predominant hatch throughout the summer. A size 14 to 16 rust-colored Elk Hair Caddis, or other dry caddis imitation is hard to beat.

Pale morning duns (PMDs) are a major hatch during late June and are overlapped by the Trico hatch, which peaks in late August and is nothing short of phenomenal. Clouds of Tricos appear at times, and any stage of this insect can cause a frenzy. Anglers should come prepared with emergers, duns, spinners and spent spinners.

By late August, casting a hopper imitation along the bank is productive, especially on windy days. Good hopper fishing can be found through September.

Some of the largest Missouri River fish are taken on streamers during the fall months. Big (size 2-6) Woolly Buggers, Matukas, Zonkers and sculpin imitations fished on sinking-tip lines is an effective way to approach fall fish—especially the monster pre-spawn browns. October and November are the hot months.

With the exception of fishing streamers, tackle for the Missouri should be delicate. Spring-creek gear is quite at home here for most of the dry-fly fishing. Since small flies and light tippets are the rule, medium-action rods with soft tips will protect those hair-like 6X tippets, which are often required.

Wading, and some bank angling, is available on the Missouri during the low-water periods, but the floating angler has the definite advantage. There are no particular hazards other than those that come with floating in general, and the Missouri is suitable for all types of boats. Driftboats and other flat-bottomed boats are the most popular because you can anchor them, but rafts and small personal boats are also used here.

There are several boat launches along the prime trout water of the Missouri. Popular floats include Holter Dam to Wolf

Fishing the Trico hatch in a side channel of the Missouri.

HEADWATERS VIEWPOINT

This point marks the beginning of the Missouri-Mississippi River drainage, the longest river system in North America.

THREE FORKS POST-1810

On the point of land between the Madison and Jefferson Rivers, trappers of the Missouri Fur Company built the Three Forks Post in 1810. All traces have since been obliterated by the annual flooding of the rivers.

Marker at Headwaters State Park, at the confluence of the Gallatin, Madison and Jefferson rivers—forming the Missouri.

Creek, Wolf Creek to Craig, Craig to the Dearborn River, and the Dearborn River to Pelican Point. There are more launches than these and, of course, you modify your float to suite how much time you have and to your desires.

A good way to approach Missouri trout while floating is to spot a pod of feeding fish and anchor well away from them. Cast your offering to the fish rising on the outside of the pod. If you cast in to the middle you will likely turn the whole pod off, and you just as well move on. Although this is a big river, the Missouri can be just as difficult and demanding as any spring creek.

As with most rivers, hiring a guide is the best way to learn the Missouri. The town of Craig has a fly shop (Missouri River Trout Shop (800) 337-8528 and the folks there can recommend reputable guides working the river. Camping is available in Craig and at the Wolf Creek Bridge.

The Missouri River is reached by taking Interstate 15 north from Butte. Access to the river is from any of the roads exiting the freeway, which parallels the river.

Little Prickly Pear Creek

For small-stream fanatics that don't mind dodging rattlesnakes, Little Prickly Pear Creek just might be up your alley. This Missouri River tributary is a beautiful, trout-filled stream that, while not a major destination water, it is a nice diversion from the big Missouri.

Beginning with the opener in May, this little stream kicks out rainbow and brown trout to 20 inches—sizable for a stream this small. During the summer months a variety of mayflies and caddis hatch. Anglers can do well with the standards though; Elk Hair Caddis, Adams and hopper patterns. The stream closes in the fall to protect the spawning browns working up from the Missouri.

Fly fishing small streams always demands patience, casting skill and a pile of flies. The vegetation around Little Prickly Pear Creek ensures this pretty little stream is no exception.

To reach Little Prickly Pear, follow the Sieben Canyon Road off I15. This road parallels much of the creek. Keep in mind that permission must be granted to fish on the private property found on the upper creek.

Canyon Ferry Reservoir

Montana is blessed (if you look at it that way) with many reservoirs that are great trout fisheries. Most of these reservoirs dam famous rivers which is not real great in some ways but that's the way it is. When rivers are swollen during the spring runoff, many of these reservoirs are in their prime. Canyon Ferry Reservoir is no exception.

Canyon Ferry Reservoir is located just east of Helena, along the Missouri River. This 25-mile-long reservoir hosts Eagle Lake rainbows, a fast-growing, long-living strain. During May, anglers can expect to catch a pile of 2- to 5-pound rainbows casting along the shores of this reservoir.

The best places to prospect are the gravel shorelines. The bays on the north end of the lake are good places to start looking. Pre-spawn rainbows will concentrate along the gravel areas, and by simply walking the shoreline, anglers can spot cruising fish. Once fish are located you can usually stay put, as there are likely plenty of fish in the same area.

A good technique for these fish is to cast Egg Sucking Leeches, Woolly Buggers and other streamers on a sinking-tip line. A short leader and tippet tapered to 1X or 2X are the most practical. The fishing remains good until the first part of June when the fish move back to deeper water.

Sun River

Although not a major destination for traveling anglers, the Sun is worthy of mention—just in case you happen to be in the area. The North Fork begins on the eastern edge of the Bob Marshall Wilderness and is joined by the South Fork at Gibson Reservoir. It then flows through a series of diversion dams en route to the Missouri and joins this great river near Great Falls, a total distance of roughly 100 miles.

Above Gibson Reservoir, the Sun hosts rainbow, cutthroat and brook trout—not monsters, but plenty of them. Below the reservoir you can add brown trout to the mix, and some of them do get big.

However, the many diversions on the Sun take their toll on the trout. It sounds like a broken record, talking about the evils of agricultural dewatering in Montana rivers, but it is a big deal, and is certainly a big deal on the Sun. Below Gibson

Reservoir the river backs up at Diversion Dam, which feeds Pishkin and Willow Creek reservoirs. Along its course, the Sun is diverted at no fewer than six diversion dams.

Below the reservoirs, the Sun flows through a steep canyon. This is probably your best bet for the largest trout. Pools, riffles, pocket water, flats—you will find it all here. Nymphs and streamers work well, as do the standard dry flies, during a hatch.

To reach Sun River, take Sun River Road from Augusta. The road parallels the canyon and takes you to Gibson Reservoir. From here, trails lead upstream.

Smith River

Many would argue that Smith River is the most scenic and secluded trout fishery in the state. The most productive trout water is the 61-mile stretch between Camp Baker and Eden Bridge, the standard float on this river. Anglers apply with Fish, Wildlife and Parks months in advance for a permit to float this section of the Smith—only nine launches per day are allowed.

The attraction is the solitude. Once you launch you are committed to the entire 61 miles (4 or 5 days). Magnificent beauty and the abundant rainbow and brown trout (more browns than rainbows) certainly add to the attraction. The trout are not monsters by Montana standards (a really good one is 20 inches) but there are plenty of them.

The Smith River begins with the confluence of the North and South Forks near White Sulphur Springs. It flows for over 100 miles through mountain valleys, ranchland and steep-walled canyons before emptying into the Missouri River, near Ulm.

This is a year-round fishery, but several factors should be considered when planning a trip. For instance, the winter months bring frigid temperatures to this area, and ice jams certainly are not conducive to river floating. Spring runoff can turn the river into a fast-paced, fishless cruise, and severe dewatering by irrigators can turn your float into a boat-dragging nightmare. It is wise to check the current conditions with FWP just before your planned float. Historically, the best times for consistent and adequate water flows are in the spring before runoff and during fall after irrigation demands have lessened. However, during heavy snow years, the entire summer can be perfect for floating.

Hatches on the Smith are varied and consistent. Stoneflies and *Baetis* in the spring provide most of the action, followed by a heavy salmonfly hatch in late May through early June. Other stoneflies, including the golden stone, and various mayflies as well as caddis and hoppers follow. In short, when approaching this river (as with any river) it is the wise angler who arrives with a variety of fly patterns. In the Smith, don't forget the big stuff either—Buggers, Zonkers, Spuddlers, etc.

Opposite page: Rock formations along the Missouri River, near Wolf Creek.
Below: Fall on the Smith River during an extremely low-water year.

Streamside thistle.

In addition to the private launches each day, outfitters are allowed nine launches per week. Guided trips can be arranged at fly shops in Helena or Great Falls. Shuttles can also be arranged. When floating the Smith, anglers are required to stay in preselected campsites. To inquire about permits contact the FWP office in Great Falls, P.O. Box 6610, Great Falls, MT 59406, (406) 454-5840.

Marias River

If you ever find yourself in Shelby, Montana—maybe returning from the Blackfeet Reservation or Alberta's Bow River, and if big brown trout get you all fired up, a few hours of your time could well be spent on the Marias River.

Not a beautiful river, not a destination—heck, not even loaded with fish, -but the Marias does have a significant population of large brown trout, fish that often top the scales at 10 pounds or better. And browns like that are certainly worth a side trip—at least for me.

The Marias River flows from Tiber Reservoir and travels roughly 80 miles before joining the Missouri near Fort Benton. However, it is only the first 10 miles of river that are cool enough to support trout, and it is this section where you will find a smattering of rainbows and the bulk of the brown trout, which average a few pounds.

Over the years the Marias and its fish have been plagued with erratic water flows, but recent minimum flow requirements have been helping this fishery out. Since it is a tailwater fishery, the fishing remains constant throughout the season. The river is open the entire year but winters in these parts are cold, only a handful of anglers venture to the Marias during winter.

Dry flies will take trout at times on the Marias but large streamers are the real meat and potatoes here. Don't be afraid to throw size 2 or 4 Muddlers, Spuddlers, Zonkers, Woolly Buggers or Matukas at these fish. Big browns get that way by eating big stuff. There is a healthy population of sculpins in this river—and browns love sculpins. Sinking-tip lines are the rule.

To reach Tiber Reservoir take Highway 2 from Shelby and turn south on the Tiber Road. Access is obvious from smaller roads once you get near the reservoir. Floating and wading are both popular here, the floater having a definite advantage.

Madison River

There is probably no river in Montana (or the United States, for that matter) more famous than the Madison. This Montana icon is routinely fabled in every sporting magazine in the country. The number of anglers who annually descend on the Madison is staggering. It was the Madison River that brought national attention to whirling disease, a problem that has reduced the rainbow trout population there drastically. Still, the Madison remains one of the best trout fisheries in the country.

The Madison begins in Yellowstone National Park at the confluence of the Gibbon and Firehole rivers. After the river leaves the Park, the Madison flows through Hebgen Lake and Quake Lake, on to Ennis Lake where it eventually merges with the Gallatin and Jefferson rivers some 140 miles from its beginning to form the Missouri River.

Bull elk in the Madison River just inside Yellowstone National Park.

Floating "The 50-mile Riffle" of the Madison River.

area for winter fishing. Any break in the cold can produce midge hatches worth taking advantage of. A good point of access is at the Raynolds Pass Bridge. From here, anglers can either walk up or downstream.

The most popular section of the Madison is the stretch below Quake Lake, where the river shoots from the mountains down to Varney Bridge, an area widely known as "The 50-mile Riffle." The river in this stretch appears, strangely enough, as one big riffle. Close inspection reveals much more. There are enough riffles, flats, pools, channels and pocket water to keep everybody happy.

From the Montana border, the Madison flows only a short distance through Yellowstone National Park, where it exits and quickly finds Hebgen Lake. This part of the Madison, although not as famous as the lower reaches, is an interesting fishery that deserves mention. The area just inside the Park boundary is accessed from the West Entrance Road. The river follows the road for a few miles here, providing access, but is often crowded. Tourists take advantage of the easy access and, although fishing can be great during a good hatch, often it is slow. The exception would be during fall (September and October) when the pre-spawn brown trout head upstream from Hebgen Lake. At this time, large streamers such as the Muddler, Clouser, Woolly Bugger, Girdle Bug and the Zonker work well.

Just outside the Park, the river can be accessed from the Highway 191 Bridge, just north of West Yellowstone. Walking upstream will take you to a few prime sections of river. Here the water is slow; hatches are consistent, reliable and small. It is important to keep in mind that this is grizzly country. If you decide to brave the fishing, make plenty of noise!

The river from Hebgen Lake down to Quake Lake is a short (1.5 miles) stretch that gets pounded by tourists staying in the local campgrounds. This area is a fantastic place to fish if your query is whitefish, but poor if your after trout. Of course, there are exceptions. The stretch just above Quake Lake is often good during the late evening for feeding fish coming up out of the lake. Likewise, during spring and fall, spawning rainbows and browns move from the lake following that powerful urge.

From Quake Lake down to Lyons Bridge, wading anglers do well, and this area is favored for its diversity. When it is open (check current regulations) it is a great

Above: Ken Bamford fishing the Madison below Hebgen Lake.
Overleaf: Angling the stretch of the Madison between
Hebgen and Quake Lake.

Madison River near West Yellowstone.

Floating is the most popular way to fish this section of the Madison. That's not to say that wade-fishing is not productive. This entire stretch of the Madison is suitable to all types of fishing styles and techniques—float, wade, dry fly, nymph, streamer, whatever-you can do it effectively here.

The salmonfly hatch creates a circus atmosphere when they appear in late June, but the hatch is brief. Various stoneflies and mayflies hatch during the summer but the meat-and-potatoes bug on this stretch of the Madison is the caddisfly. Summertime anglers should bring a variety of Elk Hair Caddis and Sparkle Pupas in sizes 12 to 18.

Varney Bridge to Ennis Lake is ideal wading water. There are many braids, pools and tailouts perfectly suited for this type of fishing. Floating is not allowed from Ennis to Ennis Lake because of the braids and associated hazards (logjams). Late fall will see some large brown trout move into this section out of Ennis Lake.

Just below Ennis Lake the Madison flows through Beartrap Canyon. This is dangerous water that should only be attempted by serious whitewater rafters—not your average fly fisher. You can walk down into the canyon but fishing is limited once you get there.

The lower Madison, below Beartrap Canyon, is slower and flatter than the upper river. Summer temperatures are often too high for productive trout fishing. The best time to hit this stretch is during the off-season—late fall, winter and early spring.

All facilities are located in West Yellowstone and in Ennis. Several fly shops and guide services can be found in each town. Camping is available in the area also. Visitors should be prepared for all types of weather. Summer snowstorms are not uncommon!

South Fork of the Madison River

The South Fork of the Madison River flows into the South Fork Arm of Hebgen Lake. There is a gravel road along the lower reaches of the river providing access to anglers, and also access to the South Fork Campground.

Although the river hosts rainbows, brookies, cutthroat, browns and whitefish, it really isn't that good for large fish during the summer months. The mouth of the South Fork is another story. During the summer, "gulper" fishing in Hebgen Lake is very popular, and the mouth of the South Fork is a prime spot to target these large feeders.

Fall will bring large browns on their spawning run into the South Fork, and large streamers will take their share of these.

Opposite page: Madison River with Madison Range in background.

A Madison rainbow comes to net.

Hebgen Lake

The word "gulper," when it refers to large trout sucking bugs off the surface of a lake originated on Hebgen Lake. During the summer (late July and August), Trico and *Callibaetis* mayflies create a predictable daily feeding of the lake's trout. It begins with the Tricos around 7 A.M., and by late morning you also have the *Callibaetis* creating a frenzy. It all ends by noon or so, when, also predictably, the wind picks up.

Fishing over the "gulpers" requires long leaders (12 to 16 feet) and fine tippets of 5X or 6X. Delicate Trico patterns, Parachute Adams, Callibaetis Cripples, Pheasant Tail Nymphs and local designs work well. The best patterns for this fishing will come from any of the several fly shops located in West Yellowstone—something definitely worth checking out.

The best "gulper" fishing will be found in the Madison Arm and the South Fork Arm. Some bank and wade fishing is possible, but float tubes and boats are the best way to get to the risers. Float tubes are the most practical as you can launch them anywhere you see rising fish.

The summer "gulper" fishing is not the only fly angling to be had on this big lake. Spring fishing in the various bays can be productive for rainbows and the fall angling at the mouths of streams emptying into the lake can be fantastic for pre-spawn browns. Some of the most productive fishing is done with big streamers.

Opposite page: Fall streamer fishing on Duck Creek.
Below: Duck Creek near its confluence with Hebgen Lake.

Sudden snowstorms can occur any time of the year in Montana's higher elevations.

Keep in mind that Hebgen is a big lake and that the wind can whip up in an instant. Take caution when and where you launch your watercraft.

Hebgen Lake is located along Highway 287 near West Yellowstone. All services and several fly shops are located in West Yellowstone. There is plenty of camping in the area.

Duck Creek

Duck Creek is a beautiful little stream that empties into the Grayling Arm of Hebgen Lake, near the junctions of Highway 287 and Highway 191, near West Yellowstone. It flows from Yellowstone National Park through brushy, swampy flatland and is difficult to fish. Those who do fight these obstacles are rewarded with plenty of smallish rainbows, brookies, cutthroat, browns and whitefish.

The real treasure of this little stream comes during the fall when large browns head up from Hebgen lake. A Girdle Bug drifted around a bend or through a pool can produce some exciting results. Besides the thick brush, there is another problem with fishing here—grizzly bears. Be careful!

Cougar Creek

Cougar Creek merges with Duck Creek a mile or so from Hebgen Lake. Like Duck Creek, Cougar also holds smallish rainbows, browns, cutthroat, brookies, grayling and whitefish. Also like Duck Creek, the stream is small, brushy, swampy and infested with grizzly bears and mosquitoes. All of these superficial miseries can surely be overlooked during the fall, when the big browns head up from Hebgen Lake to spawn.

Cliff And Wade Lake

Cliff and Wade lakes are reached by a good gravel road off Highway 287 along the Madison River west of Quake Lake. These lakes are close enough to the Madison River, and the West Yellowstone area that many visiting anglers often take advantage of these productive still waters when visiting these parts.

Cliff Lake is a narrow, 4-mile-long lake hosting rainbows, cutthroat and brookies. The clear, green water and surrounding mountains contribute to this lake's appeal. Trout cruise the drop-offs in search of whatever foods they can find. Monsters you won't find here, but plenty of fish and beautiful scenery you will. There is a campground right along the lake.

Wade Lake is located just to the west of Cliff Lake. Although it is only a mile and a half long, by a half-mile wide, this lake holds some awfully large trout. In fact, Wade Lake

Cow moose feeding in a pond near West Yellowstone.

Hook-up on Cliff Lake.

held the Montana state-record brown trout, caught back in 1967, which tipped the scale at 29 pounds.

Rainbows and browns (to 10 pounds) are caught often enough in Wade Lake to make this a destination for trophy hunters. Shorelines are steep, and bank angling is next to impossible. Float tubes or boats are a must.

Fish the drop-offs and down deep for the largest fish. Big Woolly Buggers and other streamers fished slowly along the bottom take the trophies. A boat launch is located on the east end of the lake.

Quake Lake

In 1959 an earthquake registering 7.8 on the Richter Scale rumbled through the Yellowstone area. The section of river known as the Madison Canyon, below the dam on Hebgen Lake, was changed forever. A portion of a mountain, an estimated 80 million tons of rock and earth, swept across the Madison Canyon and up the other side, much like an avalanche of snow does in the winter. Sixteen people lost their lives.

The Madison River was completely choked off and a lake began to form. The river downstream all but dried up and thousands of fish died before a channel could be cut through the debris. The result of the landslide created Quake Lake, which is now 4 miles long, 1,800 feet wide and 180 feet deep.

The Madison Canyon stretch of the river was a remarkable piece of water known for large rainbows and browns. The present lake contains rainbow, brown and cutthroat trout, as well as whitefish. Trout to five pounds are not uncommon.

Dead treetops rise from the lake's surface along the edges and these areas provide great cover for the trout. The usual array of stillwater insects can be found here, with decent hatches of mayflies and caddisflies. Nymphs fished around the structure are often productive.

There is a boat ramp located on the east end of the lake, which was once a section of the highway.

Gallatin River

It was William Clark who named the Gallatin, after Thomas Jefferson's Secretary of the Treasury, Albert Gallatin. With its beginnings in Yellowstone National Park, the Gallatin River flows in a northerly direction, roughly 100 miles to its confluence with the Madison and Jefferson rivers to create the Missouri.

The Gallatin is a small river by Montana standards, and it is not known as a big trout destination. However, it is an excellent trout stream, and is one of the prettiest (if not the prettiest) rivers in the state.

From Yellowstone Park downstream to Big Sky, the Gallatin meanders through open meadows, offering plenty of undercut banks, riffles and pools. This is great dry-fly water. Any properly fished attractor such as a Humpy or Royal Trude, or terrestrials, like hoppers and ants are seldom refused. This is especially true during mid to late summer, when floating a hopper pattern along the banks is most effective. ·

The trout you find in this stretch of the Gallatin will be rainbows, browns or cutthroat in the 10- to 15-inch range, with a 15-incher on the top end of the scale. Not monsters by Montana standards, but plentiful, hard-fighting and easy to fool.

Taylor Creek enters the Gallatin in this upper stretch, and during runoff (May and June) and at times of thunderstorms, this tributary will muddy the entire river downstream. The water above Taylor Creek often gets crowded when this is the case.

From Big Sky downstream to just past the mouth of Spanish Creek the river flows through what is commonly known as the Gallatin Canyon, approximately 20 miles in length. The river winds and twists through a canyon of steep cliffs and lodgepole pine, and is closely paralleled by Highway 191, providing great access.

The canyon water is fast-paced with plenty of pools, riffles and pocket water—ideal for short-line nymphing. This

Ken Bamford brings a rainbow to hand at the confluence of the Madison and Quake Lake.

Fishing the Madison River at the head of Quake Lake.

Above: Gallatin River Canyon during winter.
Opposite page: Fishing the Gallatin River.

stretch of river will produce rainbows and browns that can reach 18 to 20 inches, but most fall considerably short of that length.

For the largest trout on the Gallatin, the lower river from the mouth of the canyon to Three Forks (the junction with the Madison and Jefferson) is the place to be. The problem

Bison along the upper Gallatin.

though, is that the river flows through private property through this stretch. Access can be obtained at any bridge crossing, and as long as you stay below the high-water mark, Montana's stream-access law allows you to walk the stream.

Rainbows and browns of considerable size can be taken on this lower section of stream. This area is especially good during fall when brown trout migrate on their spawning run. Large streamers are the ticket.

The East Gallatin River merges with the main Gallatin below the town of Belgrade, just above the Nixon Bridge. Access here is at the Four Corners Fishing Access Site near Manhattan, the Nixon Bridge and the Logan Bridge. The usual takeout is at the ramp located in Headwaters State Park on the Missouri River, just below the mouth of the Gallatin. During fall, some very large rainbow and brown trout are taken in this section, by anglers who pound the banks with big nymphs and streamers.

The entire Gallatin has numerous and abundant hatches of the usual river insects. Anglers should go well prepared with a variety of dries, nymphs, streamers, terrestrials and attractors. Lines from full-floating to full-sinking will be helpful. Rods in the 4- to 6-weight range are adequate.

The Gallatin is reached by taking the Belgrade exit off Interstate 90 northwest of Bozeman, or by following Highway 191 north from West Yellowstone. Motels, fly shops and

guides are available in West Yellowstone, Big Sky and Bozeman. Camping is available along the Gallatin Canyon.

East Gallatin River

The East Gallatin flows for roughly 30 miles from its source in the Bridger Range to its confluence with the Gallatin near Manhattan. This is probably one of the least-known rivers in Montana—not because the fishing is poor (quite to the contrary) but probably due to the horrible access. Private land borders most of this river, and gaining access is a pain. There are bridge crossings which allow anglers access, but it's tough going, except during periods of low water.

Your best bet is to float the river but without public access areas, again, bridges are your best entry points. For this reason, small personal boats are best—something you can shoulder. If you do float, be aware of fences that cross the river.

This fertile river has a wide range of hatches. Anglers should go prepared with the usual dries and nymphs throughout the season. There is great hopper action on the East Gallatin during August and September. Fall is streamer time for the big browns—Muddlers, Spuddlers, Zonkers, Matukas, Buggers—you get the picture. Fish big streamers through the deeper holes, along banks and tailouts and hold onto your shorts!

To reach the East Gallatin take the Belgrade exit off Interstate 90. Access the river from bridges or put on your best begging face and plead with landowners.

Yellowstone River

With its beginnings high in the mountains of Yellowstone National Park, the Yellowstone flows roughly 670 miles to its confluence with the Missouri in North Dakota. There are no dams on the river, it is not dewatered during summer and it is stuffed with cutthroat, rainbow and brown trout. Access is good all along its length, it's easy to float and the surrounding scenery is spectacular. Sound like heaven? It is!

The Yellowstone is formed from melting snow and geysers in the park, runoff from the Gallatin and Absaroka mountains and from numerous tributaries. From the Yellowstone cutthroat found in the headwaters, to the rainbows and browns of Paradise Valley and beyond, the Yellowstone offers a diversity not found in many Montana rivers. This river is truly one of the West's best fisheries.

In its headwaters in Yellowstone National Park the Yellowstone River offers hike-in fishing for some of the best cutthroat angling you can find anywhere. The cutthroat, not real fussy by nature, will take nearly any dry fly tossed at them. Also in the park Yellowstone Lake and Buffalo Ford on the mainstem Yellowstone offer spectacular angling, again for the Yellowstone cutthroat.

Yellowstone River near Big Timber.

Thunderhead brewing over the Yellowstone River.

When the river leaves the Park at Gardiner it is a rough, tumbling river through Yankee Jim Canyon. Fishing can be good in this big, deep water, but there is little wading. Most angling is done with big nymphs cast against the shore or into pockets. There are Class III rapids in Yankee Jim Canyon, and floating should not be attempted by those without the proper skills.

Once the river leaves the canyon it flows north through Paradise Valley, which is quite possibly the prettiest section of the Yellowstone. Here the river is paralleled by Highway 89, with plenty of access points along the way. The Absaroka Mountains tower to the east, and the river winds gently through the valley to Livingston. This is the most popular section of the Yellowstone, for both floating and wading anglers.

At Livingston the river turns to the east, gains volume and eventually slows. Good trout fishing continues to Big Timber and beyond but eventually the Yellowstone becomes too warm to support trout of significant numbers.

Timing is everything when planning a trip to the Yellowstone River. The fishing can be good in the upper river even during winter. March will often see great midge hatches, followed by *Baetis*, and March browns in April and into early May. Late April will also see the beginning of the famous "Mother's Day Hatch" (Grannom caddis). Any time after the first week in May the yearly runoff can blow the entire river out. Depending on the amount of winter snow, this can last into July or even longer in particularly heavy snowfall years. Fishing is pretty much a bust during this time, with the exception of the salmonfly hatch which occurs in mid-June. Big stonefly nymphs cast tight to the shore will work—even when the water is brown.

If the river clears in early July, salmonflies will still be present and adults as well as nymphs will work well. Also in the water at this time will be golden stones, yellow sallies, green drakes and caddisflies. It is the caddisfly that is the major hatch during the summer months. Anglers should have a variety of caddis imitations, including cased larve, pupas and adults.

Perhaps the most funtime on the Yellowstone River is during August and September when hoppers make their appearance. Floating the river during the mellow flow and casting your favorite hopper imitation to the bank is hard to beat.

Baetis make a showing again in the fall, and streamers will take their share of fish too. Big, pre-spawn browns are especially likely to take a Muddler, Spuddler, Bugger or other big (size 2 or 4) streamer that swims past.

The hub of the Yellowstone River is the town of Livingston. Here you will find several fly shops, including the

Overleaf: Sunset on the Yellowstone River.
Below: Yellowstone River near Gardiner.

Yellowstone River in Paradise Valley.

Large stonefly nymphs are great both before and after the salmonfly hatch.

famous Dan Bailey's Fly Shop. Many more shops are in the area, and guides from all over this part of Montana run clients on this famous river. All services, including camping, can be found along the Yellowstone.

To reach the upper Yellowstone River and Paradise Valley, exit Interstate 90 at Livingston and follow Highway 89 south, paralleling the river all the way to the Yellowstone National Park entrance. The river below Livingston can be accessed off Interstate 90 in several places. Public access points, are well marked, for the most part.

Paradise Valley Spring Creeks

It would be safe to say that the most famous spring creeks in the West are those found in Paradise Valley, south of Livingston. The names, Armstrong, Nelson's and DePuy are music to the ears of spring-creek fanatics—those who enjoy fishing tiny flies on tiny tippets to incredibly difficult trout, and don't mind paying a daily fee to do so. No, the Paradise Valley spring creeks are not for everyone.

Armstrong and DePuy spring creeks are located on the west side of the Yellowstone River, just south of Livingston. Nelson's is found on the east side of the river. All of these spring creeks host a healthy supply of rainbows and browns.

Spring creeks, by nature, are clear, have relatively stable water temperatures and have incredible hatches of insects—often very small insects. Hatches frequently overlap and it is difficult to figure out just what the trout are feeding on. Anglers should come prepared with a variety of small mayfly and caddis imitations in all stages of their life cycle, as well as scuds, midges, ants, leeches and a positive attitude. Fine tippets (7X are common) add to the challenge of taking a three- or four-pound trout from these creeks.

One of the biggest challenges on these spring creeks is getting a reservation to fish, as they book early during the prime fishing season. Livingston area fly shops book and guide the spring creeks, or you can call them direct: Nelson's (406) 222-2159; Armstrong's (406) 222-2974; DePuy's (406) 222-0211.

Big Spring Creek

Although Big Spring Creek is a genuine spring creek, rushing from the ground at 64,000 gallons a minute, it doesn't appear as most other western spring creeks. It does not flow lazily along with constant hatches of tiny bugs. It is not crystal-clear all the time—in fact, it experiences the spring runoff and muddies after a good storm from its tributaries. But it does, however, hold trout that are spring-creek spooky, spring-creek demanding and of spring-creek size.

Big Spring Creek begins in the hills southeast of Lewistown. It travels 31 miles to its confluence with the Judith River. The creek runs right through Lewistown, and a road leading through town follows the creek along most of its best fishing. There is plenty of access for the wading angler.

The upper reaches, downstream from the Big Spring Trout Hatchery, is characterized by riffles, pools and under-

Spring creek brown.

cut brushy banks. This is a great place to drift a nymph or cast a dry fly when rising trout so warrant. Rainbow and brown trout are both found in this stretch.

The lower reaches of Big Spring Creek (below Lewistown) flow through rangeland, are slower and hold more browns than rainbows. Attention should always be paid to hatches, but streamers and hoppers tossed along the grassy banks are often very effective.

Several insects are important here throughout the season. Midges in the winter and early spring, a few mayflies, the most important being the pale morning dun during summer but it is the caddisfly that is the most consistent, and most important adult insect here. Anglers should, in addition to a good supply of small nymphs, carry at least the basic, spring creek selection of dry flies.

Floating lines and a 3- to 4-weight rod is all that's needed here, except during fall streamer fishing for the big browns. A mini sinking-tip will allow you to dredge the deeper pools and banks.

Big Spring Creek is reached by taking Highway 191 north from Big Timber to Moore, then Highway 87 east from Moore to Lewistown.

Musselshell River

Like so many Montana rivers that flow through ranchland, over the years the Musselshell has been victim to irresponsible dewatering during summer, irresponsible grazing practices along its banks and general disregard when it comes to its fish. The results of this neglect are especially felt during successive drought years. Fortunately, as I write this, we are in a wet trend and the trout are rebounding.

With its headwaters in the Crazy Mountains, the Musselshell travels through the rolling hills in its upper stretches, then through cattle country for much of its 365-mile length before emptying into Fort Peck Reservoir. The upper reaches host rainbow, brown and cutthroat trout. Brown trout are the attraction in the prime water from the Selkirk public access near Martinsdale down to Harlowton. The lower reaches of the river contain several warmwater species.

Besides the dewatering problems in the Musselshell, access is a major obstacle for anglers. Most of the river travels through private land. This is not to say that a friendly permission-seeking visit to local ranchers will be met with a denial—

most often you are granted right of passage. But there are few public access points.

The Selkirk access near Martinsdale is probably the best choice for floating or wading anglers. Access is also available at the Highway 191 bridge south of Harlowton. Working your way upstream or downstream from either access point puts you on some good water.

You will not find tons of brown trout in this river, however many of the fish you do find will be big. For this reason, the Musselshell has a devoted following of "hog hunters." Trout of over 5 pounds are taken from this river by persistent and knowledgeable anglers.

As with many "big brown" streams, one of the most effective methods for taking these fish is with streamers—Muddlers, Zonkers, Buggers and the like. This is not big water, so shorter rods will work best. Weighted flies or short sinking-tips are the ticket.

The Musselshell is reached by taking Highway 191 off Interstate 90 at Big Timber. Follow Highway 191 to Harlowton. U.S. 12 follows the river for much of its fishable length.

Stillwater River

The fast-paced Stillwater River comes to life high in the rugged Beartooth Mountains north of Yellowstone Park. Its cascading waters descend from the mountains and eventually join the Yellowstone River near Columbus. Throughout most of its course, the Stillwater is a clear, rambling stream with a good population of trout.

The upper reaches of the Stillwater host mostly brook trout, but cutthroat and rainbow trout are also available. A twelve-incher is a whopper. The best way to approach these fish (Woodbine-Stillwater Trail) is by casting a Humpy, Royal Coachman, Adams or Elk Hair Caddis into the pockets and pools.

The middle section of the Stillwater is approached near the town of Nye. The West Fork adds volume here, and rainbow and brown trout become more predominant. The river is still fast here and becomes a classic mountain stream in appearance. Dries, streamers and nymphs are all popular in this section.

The lower river, from Absarokee to the confluence with the Yellowstone, holds the largest fish. The Rosebud River enters at Absarokee, adding volume, and the river slows. There are some public access points but the lower river travels through a good deal of private, posted land. Anglers destined to fish the lower river should bone up on their permission-asking skills.

Stillwater River.

Farmland along the Shields River with the Crazy Mountains in the distance.

The Stillwater River is reached by taking the Columbus exit off Interstate 90, following Highway 78 to Absarokee, and then following Highway 420 to Nye and beyond.

Shields River

Flowing from the Crazy Mountains, the Shields River travels roughly 60 miles to its confluence with the Yellowstone River east of Livingston. There is some Yellowstone cutthroat fishing in the upper reaches, but this small, winding river really shines in its lower reaches for brown trout, especially browns that migrate up from the Yellowstone in fall to spawn.

The big problem on the Shields is access. Almost all of the river flows through private, posted property. Access is from U.S 89, county bridges and by begging landowners. Swimming a Muddler Minnow or Woolly Bugger through a bend in this gorgeous little stream during fall is definitely worth the effort of gaining access.

A Shields River brown trout.

EASTERN Montana

Eastern Montana has little to offer the trout fly-fisher except for the Bighorn River, which is possibly the single-best trout stream in the country. The eastern regions of the state are windblown and desolate, with water temperatures much too warm for trout.

There are a few exceptions, such as the fishery found in the Missouri River below Fort Peck Reservoir, where a few devoted anglers target the big rainbows and browns found there. This is a harsh area to fish though—it's hot, and there are a pile of rattlesnakes to deal with.

Bighorn River

General George Armstrong Custer would have had a much better time chasing trout in the Bighorn River with a fly rod than chasing Indians in the hills above the river (at least, that's a personal guess). It was not far from this world-famous river that it all ended for Custer and his men back in 1876.

There is probably not one devout fly-fisher on the planet that has not heard of the Bighorn River. This is truly one of Montana's finest, and everyone should fish it at least once. The Bighorn River is the river by which all other rivers are measured.

The Bighorn flows from Bighorn Lake, just north of the Wyoming border, and travels north for roughly 84 miles before emptying into the Yellowstone River near Custer. It is the first dozen or so miles below the reservoir that is the prime trout water—that which draws anglers from around the world.

Opposite page: Brown trout.
Below: The beginning of the "famous stretch" of the Bighorn River from Yellowtail Dam.

Drifting the Bighorn.

Like many tailwater fisheries, the Bighorn is a year-round water. Relatively constant water temperatures for the first several miles of river translates into consistent hatches, many of which overlap. The most popular months on the river are April through October, but trout are certainly available during every month of the year.

Blue-winged olives begin in late April and hatch into June. A size 18 *Baetis* imitation will work well on top, Hare's Ear and Pheasant Tail Nymphs in the same size will produce subsurface. In fact, small nymphs will work any time on the Bighorn—something to remember during the lulls between hatches.

One of the most exciting hatches on the Bighorn is the pale morning dun (PMD), size 16. These mayflies are available from mid-July through August. Adult PMDs, cripples and nymphs all work well. A 5X or 6X tippet is standard when fishing PMDs, as it is for most Bighorn hatches.

Overlapping the PMDs is the black caddis, size 16. This hatch will run from mid-August through September. This hatch is overlapped by a lighter colored caddis. The bottom line is this: anglers should be prepared with a selection of Elk Hair Caddis in black to shades of brown, and in sizes 12 to 18.

After the caddis come the Tricos, then the *Baetis* again, and during the winter months it is the midge that steals the show. The midges are small (size 20 or 22) and fishing them can be frustratingly difficult. The standard patterns on the Bighorn are the Palomino Midge, Serendipity and Griffith's Gnat, all in sizes 16 to 20.

One popular pattern on this river loathed by many, praised by others-is the San Juan Worm. This fly works all year long. Tied in size 6 to 10, and in red, orange or brown, this fly is dead-drifted along the bottom with amazing results. Another "standard" to be aware of is the scud. Scuds are prevalent on the Bighorn, and a good scud imitation in size 16 or 18 is always a good choice.

When planning a trip to the Bighorn there are a few things to keep in mind. The wind can howl across the eastern Montana plains and the Bighorn area gets its share of it. In general, a 5- or 6-weight rod is ideal for the Bighorn, but if it's windy, a 7-weight might be a better choice.

Turnover of Bighorn Lake can turn things off. This generally happens in the fall but can happen earlier as well. When this happens, moss will be floating down the river, trout will be tight-lipped and your time would be better spent elsewhere. Calling area fly shops for current information is always a good idea. One source for information is Cottonwood Camp, which is located along the river, (406) 666-2391.

Another point to consider is that the Bighorn runs through the Crow Indian Reservation. You must have permission to gain bank access, and this is not an easy thing. However, the Bighorn is easy to float and this is really the best way to approach the river anyway. There are several public boat access points. The two most popular floats are from Afterbay Dam access to Three Mile access, and Three Mile Access to Bighorn access.

To reach the Bighorn River, exit Interstate 90 at Hardin and head south. Fly shops, lodges and guide services are available in Fort Smith, right along the river. Camping is available at Cottonwood Camp.

General Montana nymph selection.

A beautiful Bighorn River brown trout.

ALPINE Lakes

Montana is blessed with several mountain ranges, offering a tremendous fishery for the adventurous angler. Thousands of alpine lakes are scattered across the high country, hosting rainbow, brown, cutthroat, brook, golden and lake trout, as well as grayling. The alpine regions offer great fishing in a spectacular setting—what more could you want?

Granted, fishing the high country is not for everyone. Many of the best waters require a considerable effort to reach. Grizzly bears can be a factor in some parts of the backcountry and, typical of alpine fishing, cooperative fish are no guarantee. Snowstorms can happen any day of the year, backcountry travelers need to be aware and prepared for

this. There are many factors involved in a successful fishing trip into the mountains. One constant, though, is the gorgeous scenery you will find there.

Winterkill is another factor to deal with in the high country. Severe winters with thick, life-choking ice can kill off a shallow lake, and it will remain barren until it can be planted again. Heavy winter snows can keep trails closed and lakes frozen over until late in the season. It is advisable to call Montana Fish Wildlife and Parks (406) 444-2535 for an up-to-date report before heading into any wilderness area.

Deciding just where to start exploring the backcountry can sometimes be the biggest challenge. The best way is to

Opposite page: Absaroka Mountains.
Below: Rainbow trout from a mountain stream.

A Big Hole grayling that fell for a streamer.

decide on an area, figure out how much time you have to spend and how much energy you want to put out, get a topographical map and go from there. A good source for several destinations is the Montana Atlas & Gazetteer by the DeLorme Mapping Company. With this, the entire state, including all the backcountry, is available at your fingertips.

Once you do decide on a destination, a lightweight 3- or 4-weight rod, a floating line and a handful of flies is all you need, for the fishing anyway. Alpine trout are usually not fussy eaters. In their world, anything that moves and will fit in their mouth is food. Attractors like the Humpy and Royal Coachman are hard to beat for dry flies, along with the standards, like the Adams, Elk Hair Caddis, mosquito and Black Gnat. For nymphs, bring a selection including the Gold Ribbed Hare's Ear, Pheasant Tail, Tellico and Zug Bug.

Following are just some of the alpine fisheries available in Montana, and a very small list of the more popular lakes in some specific areas. There are literally thousands from which to choose. All one needs to do is look at a detailed map of the alpine regions of the state to get a mind-boggling idea of what is available to the adventurous hiking angler.

Bob Marshall Wilderness Complex

Of all the mountainous areas of Montana, it is the Bob Marshall, Great Bear and Scapegoat wilderness areas together (Bob Marshall Wilderness Complex) that comprise one of the largest expanses of undeveloped, roadless pieces of alpine real estate in the contiguous United States. The Bob Marshall complex runs along both sides of the Continental Divide.

Most of the fish found in the high lakes here will be cutthroat, but some lakes also host rainbow trout. Trails leading into this wilderness from the Flathead River drainages are the best fishing. Some of the more popular lakes include; Sunburst, Necklace Lakes, Lena, Pyramid, Big Salmon, Dickey, Almeda, Marion and the Tranquil Lakes.

Absaroka-Beartooth Wilderness

The Absaroka Mountains tower to the east above the Yellowstone River in Paradise Valley. These are Montana's highest mountains and access into many of the wilderness lakes is a grunt, to say the least. The fishing found in some of these lakes and the alpine setting, however, are well worth the effort.

Access into the Absarokas is via the Mill, Emigrant, Sixmile and Bear creeks trailheads, on the west side of the mountains. In these mountains the angler can find rainbow, brown, brook and golden trout. Pine Creek Lake, Knox Lake and Fish Lake are a few popular lakes with straightforward access.

On the eastern side of the mountains, access up the Boulder River will lead to several lakes in the Boulder drainage, some of which offer outstanding fishing. Some of the most popular waters include; Fish, Mirror, Rainbow, Speculator, West Boulder and Silver Lake.

The East Rosebud headwaters offer some impressive fishing. Big brown trout, rainbows and goldens can be found in some waters. A few of the popular waters include; East Rosebud Lake, Rainbow Lake, Fossil Lake and Lake at the Falls.

The Rock Creek drainage hosts several lakes with outstanding fishing. Access is by the West Fork Rock Creek Road, Lake Fork trail. Brook, cutthroat and rainbow trout are the species found here. The most popular waters include; Canyon Lake, Sliderock Lake, Hell Roaring Lakes, Moon Lake and Glacier Lake.

Pioneer Mountains

Southwest Montana's Pioneer Mountains host many easy to reach, quality fishing lakes hosting rainbow, cutthroat and brook trout, as well as grayling. In the West Pioneers, popular lakes include; Lake of the Woods, Odell Lake, Ferguson Lake, Foolhen Lake, Stone Lake, Sandy Lake and Baldy Lake. In the East Pioneers, it's Pear, Boot, Anchor, Estler, Brownes, Waukena, Tahepia, Crescent, Grayling and Canyon Lakes, to name just a few. Check out a topographical map for the possibilities and the best access.

Gallatin Range

Most of the good fly-fishing lakes in the Gallatin Range are accessed off highway 191, the Highway that travels from Bozeman to West Yellowstone. Some of the most popular are the Hidden Lakes Chain. Only five of the eight lakes hold rainbow and golden trout. Another popular chain is the Golden Trout Lakes, one of which holds cutthroat and golden trout, the others are barren.

Other popular waters in the Gallatin Range include Rat Lake, Ramshorn Lake, Mirror Lake and Spanish Lakes. There are several small lakes in the Gallatins that warrant a little exploration.

Anaconda-Pintler Wilderness

The Anaconda-Pintler Wilderness follows the Continental Divide in western Montana, and drainages from this mountainous area feed such famous waters as Rock Creek, the Big Hole and Bitterroot River. There are many alpine lakes scattered through these mountains as well, offering fine fishing to those with the ambition to find them.

Most of the best angling is accessed from Forest Service roads west of Georgetown Lake. Popular lakes here include Upper Carpp and Lower Carpp, Tamarack, Edith, Johnson, Martin and Rainbow Lake.

On the Big Hole side of the Wilderness, you will find lakes such as Mystic and Seymour, where rainbows and brookies can be found. Many more lakes also deserve attention.

On the west side of the Wilderness, the Bitterroot side, Forest Service roads turn to trails that eventually lead to lakes. Many contain trout. It's simply a matter of getting there.

Brook trout are found in many high lakes and tributaries.

Selected Fly Patterns

DRY FLIES

Ausable Wulff

Olive Humpy

Parachute Adams

Green Paradrake

Hairwing Colorado Green Drake

Thorax Callibaetis

Thorax PMD

Thorax Slate Olive

Hi-Vis Comparadun Trico

No Hackle Slate Olive

No Hackle White Black

Ho Hackle Gray Yellow

Parachute Lt. Orange

Hen Spinner Dun Brown

Cripple Pale Morning Dun

Sparkle Dun PMD

Sparkle Dun Baetis

E-Z Caddis Olive

X Caddis Olive

Hemingway Caddis

Spent Partridge Caddis Olive

Griffith's Gnat

Black Fur Ant

Foam Beetle

Stimulator Royal

Stimulator Olive

Stimulator Orange

Henry's Fork Golden Stone

Rogue Roam Stone Giant

Henry's Fork Salmon Fly

Madam X

Parachute Hopper Tan

Dave's Hopper

Turk's Tarantula Brown

for Montana Waters

NYMPHS

Palomino Midge dark olive

Palomino Midge black

Brassie

Serendipity

Telico

Bead Head Emerger BWO

Bead Head Flashback Pheasant Tail olive

Bead Head Copper John

Gold Bead Prince Nymph

Mercer's Micro Mayfly

Bead Head Emerger PMD

Caddis Emerger olive

Soft Hackle Pheasant Tail

Gold Bead Red Squirrel Nymph

Black Rubber Legs

Bead Head K. Mini Stone black

San Juan Worm red

Crane fly Larva olive

Muddler Minnow

Big horn Shrimp

Barr's Damsel olive

Bead Head Mini Leech olive

Bead Head Rubber Leg olive

Woolly Bugger black

Woolly Bugger olive

Bead Head Flashabugger

Flashabugger black

Yuk Bug

Matuka black

Matuka olive

Zonker olive

Zonker white & pearl

Matuka Sculpin gold

Zonker natural & pearl

Clouser Deep Minnow golden shiner

Selected Fly Patterns
FOR
Montana Waters

With the myriad water systems in the state—rivers, streams, lakes and ponds—the bountiful waters of the Big Sky state host virtually every species of aquatic food item and terrestrial available to trout in the West. Needless to say, the angler who visits Montana should bring plenty of flies to match a variety of food items, or plenty of credit cards or cash to buy flies at any of the numerous fly shops found in this state. No matter how many flies you bring, you will still need something you don't have and end up visiting a fly shop. Everyone knows that.

Following is a general list of useful patterns for Montana waters.

Cripple Pale Morning Dun	Sparkle Dun *Baetis*	Caddis Emerger, olive
Dave's Hopper	Spent Partridge Caddis Olive	Barr's Damsel, olive
E-Z Caddis, olive	Stimulator, green	Black Flashabugger
Foam Beetle	Stimulator, orange	Mercer's Micro Mayfly
Black Fur Ant	Stimulator, Royal	Soft Hackle Pheasant Tail
Griffith's Gnat	Thorax Callibaetis	Serendipity, dark green
Green Paradrake	Thorax PMD	Matuka Sculpin, gold
Hairwing Colorado Green Drake	Thorax Slate Olive	Matuka, olive
Hemingway Caddis	Turk's Tarantula, brown	Matuka, black
Henry's Fork Golden Stone	X Caddis, olive	Muddler Minnow
Henry's Fork Salmonfly	Ausable Wulff	Zonker, white and pearl
Henspinner, dun brown	Bead Head Copper John	Zonker, natural and pearl
Olive Humpy	Bead Head Flashabugger	Zonker, olive
Madam X	Bead Head Emerger PMD	Clouser's Deep Minnow, Golden Shiner
Hi Vis Comparadun Trico, black olive	Bead Head Emerger BWO	Woolly Bugger, black
Slate Olive No Hackle	Bead Head Flashback Pheasant Tail, olive	Woolly Bugger, olive
Gray Yellow No Hackle	Bead Head Kaufmann's Mini Stone, black	Yuk Bug
White Black No Hackle	Bead Head Mini Leech, olive	San Juan Worm, red
Parachute Adams	Bead Head Rubber Legs, olive	Palomino Midge, black
Parachute Hopper, tan	Gold Bead Prince Nymph	Palomino Midge, dark olive
Parachute, light orange	Gold Bead Red Squirrel Nymph	Cranefly Larva, olive
Rogue Foam Stone Giant	Black Rubber Legs	Brassie
Sparkle Dun PMD Yellow Olive	Bighorn Shrimp, orange	Telico

Montana
HATCH CHART

Montana waters host nearly every aquatic food item and terrestrial available to western trout. The hatches are diverse, and some fertile waters produce blinding hatches of stoneflies, mayflies and caddisflies—often overlapping. Different geographic regions experience specific hatches at different times. It would be impossible to create one hatch chart for the entire state. There are just too many factors involved. Following is a general chart of the major hatches and other food items to use as a basic timing for Montana waters. The best bet for up-to-date hatch information is to call or stop by a Montana fly shop in the area you intend to fish.

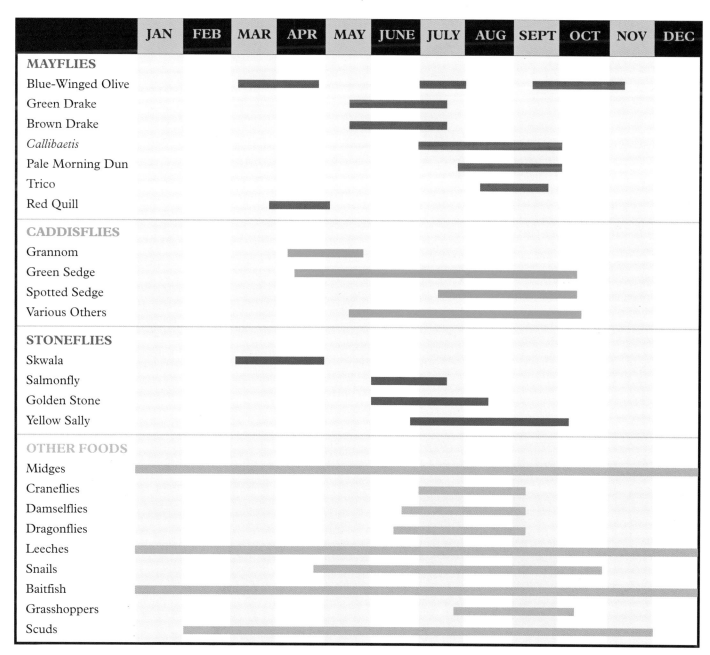

	JAN	FEB	MAR	APR	MAY	JUNE	JULY	AUG	SEPT	OCT	NOV	DEC
MAYFLIES												
Blue-Winged Olive			███	███			███			███	███	
Green Drake					███	███						
Brown Drake					███	███						
Callibaetis							███	███	███			
Pale Morning Dun								███	███			
Trico								███				
Red Quill				███								
CADDISFLIES												
Grannom				███	███							
Green Sedge				███	███	███	███	███	███	███		
Spotted Sedge							███	███	███	███		
Various Others					███	███	███	███	███	███		
STONEFLIES												
Skwala			███	███								
Salmonfly						███	███					
Golden Stone						███	███	███				
Yellow Sally							███	███	███	███		
OTHER FOODS												
Midges	███	███	███	███	███	███	███	███	███	███	███	███
Craneflies							███	███	███			
Damselflies						███	███	███				
Dragonflies						███	███	███				
Leeches	███	███	███	███	███	███	███	███	███	███	███	███
Snails					███	███	███	███	███	███		
Baitfish	███	███	███	███	███	███	███	███	███	███	███	███
Grasshoppers							███	███	███			
Scuds	███	███	███	███	███	███	███	███	███	███	███	███

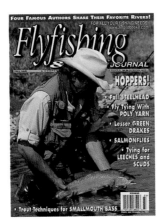